MAMUSHKA

МАМУШКА

In memory of Lusia and Zhenia, the original mamushkas

My late Grandmother Lusia
and my late Aunt Zhenia
Parizh, Ukraine, 1940

An Hachette UK Company
www.hachette.co.uk

First published in Great Britain in 2015 by
Mitchell Beazley, a division of Octopus Publishing Group Ltd
Endeavour House
189 Shaftesbury Avenue
London WC2H 8JY
www.octopusbooks.co.uk

ISBN 978 1 78472 038 4

A CIP catalogue record for this book is available from the British Library.

Printed and bound in China

10 9 8 7 6 5 4 3 2 1

Publishing Director Stephanie Jackson
Managing Editor Sybella Stephens
Senior Art Editor Juliette Norsworthy
Photographer Kris Kirkham
Food Stylist Olia Hercules
Prop Stylist Linda Berlin
Senior Production Manager Peter Hunt

MAMUSHKA

МАМУШКА

OLIA HERCULES

Mitchell Beazley

Зміст | Contents

Вступ | Introduction

Mamushka… is not actually a real word.

My brother Sasha and I watched *The Addams Family* film for the first time in 1996 (everything came about five years late in post-Soviet Ukraine). And at some point during the movie, a bunch of American actors suddenly spoke a made-up Eastern European language and danced the *mamushka* – 'the dance of brotherly love' taught to the family by their Cossack cousins. Our whole family found this part of the film irresistibly hilarious and since then my brother and I renamed our mum *Mamushka*.

I now associate the word with strong women in general, I have become a *mamushka* myself – changed careers, worked in restaurants, had a son and continue to work hard and cook incessantly.

Besides the pure 'we can do it' aspect, *mamushka* is also about the old and the new. It's about preserving culinary traditions and carrying them over into the modern world. And, boy, was my homeland of Ukraine full of diverse, incredible culinary treasures that deserve to be cherished.

I was born in 1984 in Kakhovka, Ukraine, only two hours' drive from the Crimean border. When people suggest that I must be used to the cold, I realize how inextricably bound the Western vision of Ukraine is with that of Russia – vast, grey and bleak. Yet the south of Ukraine is only an hour away from Turkey by air. Our winters are mild, our summers long and hot and our food a cornucopia of colour and flavour.

When I think of home I think of giant sunflower heads, and a pink tomato the size of a small grapefruit, with cracks in its sugary skin, ready to be torn and bathed in unrefined sunflower oil. It really was very Jonathan Safran-esque – everything was illuminated.

We grew up eating seasonally, as happily there was no alternative. I remember the aroma of the first prickly cucumber in May, my mother chopping it straight over the chipped enamel bowl, then adding the tomatoes, radishes and a whole bunch of chopped dill, all well seasoned and lightly dressed with *smetana* – the silkiest of soured creams. My favourite part of the meal was dipping a piece of bread into the pool of pink-stained leftover dressing speckled with dill

fronds and watching the pink seep into the bread.

Summers were about running through fields of sweet, moustachioed pea pods, popping fresh green morsels into our mouths until our bellies could take no more. There were geese pecking at our mulberry-stained feet, and goats that my grandmother christened with dodgy political names – one was called Hussein and the other Shevardnadze. Don't even ask.

There was green *borshch*, bursting with the malachite hue of wilted sorrel along with finely chopped spring onion, with shards of boiled egg crowning its surface. I recall sucking the nectar out of acacia and petunia blossoms, a natural outdoor sweet treat, while my aunt sprinkled fresh sour cherries with sugar and then wrapped them in the thinnest of pasta squares, ready to be plunged into a pot of boiling water – a dessert to behold! The enticing smells of warm poppy seed cakes, curd cheese biscuits, apple cakes and 'wasp nest' buns are forever fresh in my mind.

Despite my strong Ukrainian identity, I have always cherished and taken pride in the cultural diversity that we were so lucky to enjoy in Ukraine. My paternal grandmother is Siberian, my mother has Jewish and Bessarabian (Moldovan) roots, my father was born in Uzbekistan and we have Armenian relatives and Ossetian friends. This book is an ode to all those women (and men) that I was raised by and grew up with, and the food they lovingly prepared. It's food so familiar to me that I hadn't realized it was something special until I became a chef, and even more so when the conflict in Ukraine erupted, prompting me into frantically documenting the recipes that I was so scared I might suddenly lose. This is the stuff of my childhood, a life that I want to share with you in order to dispel the myths about my home country and its surrounding areas, and to give the messy geo-political mosaic a human face. As well as a rich history, culture and traditions, Ukrainians also have that great gift of adaptability and tolerance.

Having started off viewing this project as offering a journey into a little-known culinary quarter to those interested in extending their cultural horizons, when I finished it I realized that it has a universal appeal. There are light, summery dishes along with hearty dishes and broths that make you feel nourished just by inhaling their aroma. There are luscious cakes to titillate any dessert lover, and the fermenting and cheese-making recipes will interest the many permaculturalists out there. While some dishes will take time to prepare, others are gratifyingly quick. And almost all of the material comes from my family, bar a couple of my own recipes that I felt fitted well organically, as I use them a lot.

None of the recipes are prescriptive in the sense that I really hope to encourage you to adapt them to suit individual tastes, as cooking is best when done instinctively. If the dough feels too wet and soft, don't worry about what my recipe says – it may be more humid in your kitchen than it was in mine when I made it, so just add more flour. If you hate dill, simply leave it out or add another herb. Nevertheless, do give dill a try and you'll soon discover that it's not only good with fish but with many other things besides.

I hope you enjoy looking at my Ukraine through a *mamushka*'s eyes, and I hope you are beguiled by my rather eccentric family stories.

But above all, I hope you actually get to do some cooking and enjoy lots of bread dipping, be it in butter, herbs, broths or soured cream and dill.

Olushka

Some useful ingredients

Gherkins Where pickled gherkins are called for, every recipe in this book screams for proper 'fermented' gherkins (*see* page 152). If you don't make your own, look out for the word '*kiszony*' in Polish grocery shops – gherkins that have been pickled in vinegar just won't do.

Horseradish leaves, blackcurrant leaves, dill heads & sour cherry leaves These first three ingredients are the typical flavourings used in pickling in Eastern Europe, while sour cherry leaves as well as horseradish leaves have tannins so they help keep your pickles crunchy. I have seen bundles of horseradish leaves and dill heads in Polish grocery shops, but failing that, ask a friend with an allotment who may grow the plants or know someone who does, or substitute with dill stalks, mustard seeds, allspice berries or coriander seeds.

Kefir This fermented milk drink is widely used in Eastern Europe, and we often use it to make dough (*see* page 48). It should be available in Eastern European grocery shops and good supermarkets, but natural yogurt thinned down with a small amount of water is a good enough substitute. People often make it by adding a yeast starter to the milk, but my grand-mother and mother simply let the milk go sour, relying on the natural yeasts floating about the kitchen.

Margarine This is such a 1980s ingredient, I know, so please feel free to substitute the more modern, and much healthier, butter in every recipe – with the exception of the *Berlins'ke pechyvo* biscuits (*see* page 180) and the *Napoleon* cake (*see* page 188). Trust me, those two recipes are only right when a bit of margarine is thrown into the mix.

Meat I urge you to use top-quality meat, especially when making broths. The rest of the ingredients in those recipes are so cheap and so basic that it's worth investing in very, very good meat, as that's where the flavour will come from. Otherwise, you can always ask your butcher for bones, which also make a beautiful stock, and they will probably happily give them to you for free.

Parsley root looks like parsnip but is used in Eastern Europe to give stocks a strong celery and parsley aroma. I have seen it in a few Polish shops and farmers' markets, but if you cannot find it, substitute parsley stalks or carrots.

Smetana A type of soured cream, homemade Ukrainian *smetana* that you find at markets is thick and viscous and slightly golden. I buy the lighter, Polish equivalent from Eastern European grocery shops, which I actually prefer. But if you can't find that, a good-quality crème fraîche or a thick Greek yogurt would be fine instead.

Syr This is the Ukrainian version of curd cheese or quark but a lot creamier and not as dry. I have included a recipe for it (*see* page 109), for which you need to hunt down raw (unpasteurized) milk. However, Polish and other Eastern European shops sell *twaróg*, which isn't as beautiful as the homemade stuff but would work perfectly as a substitute.

Unrefined sunflower oil This has a strong fragrance of toasted sunflower seeds, almost like sesame seed oil. We don't cook with it; we only use it for dressings. I bring back to the UK the stuff that my grandmother buys from a factory located directly opposite her house in Voznesenk. But if you don't have a Ukrainian babushka, do not despair – Clearspring produce a slightly milder version, which is equally beautiful.

супи
Broths & Soups

My uncle in Moscow would often be asked by his Russian friends: 'Is it true that Ukrainians eat *borshch* three times a day?' He answered, 'If you guys could make a proper Ukrainian *borshch*, you would get up at night to eat it.' Stock is very important here, as with every other broth recipe in this book, and the meat that you use should be well marbled, otherwise it will never become meltingly soft. The most authentic of *borshches* should include pork *salo* (cured pork belly, *see* page 136) minced with garlic and added at the end. A skinny, old boiling chicken also makes a flavoursome *borshch*.

Борщ | *Borshch*
Ukrainian beetroot broth

Serves 4

200g (7oz) beetroot, peeled and cut
    into matchsticks
200g (7oz) potatoes, peeled and chopped
2 tablespoons sunflower oil
I onion, finely chopped
I carrot, peeled and roughly grated
I red pepper, cored, deseeded
    and chopped
I tablespoon tomato purée
I beef tomato (skin discarded), roughly
    grated, or 100g (3½ oz) fermented
    tomatoes (*see* page 157)
½ small white cabbage, shredded
400g (13oz) can red kidney beans,
    drained and rinsed
sea salt flakes and freshly ground
    black pepper

Stock

500g (1lb) oxtail or fatty beef short ribs
I onion, peeled but kept whole
I bay leaf
2.5 litres (4 pints) cold water

To serve

100ml (3½fl oz) soured cream
½ bunch of dill, chopped
Pampushky (*see* page 42)

I To make the stock, simply place the meat, whole onion, bay leaf and measurement water in a large saucepan. Season the water lightly and cook over a low heat for I hour. Skim off the scum with a spoon from time to time.

2 Add the beetroot and potatoes to the stock, season well with salt and pepper and cook over low heat for 30 minutes.

3 Meanwhile, heat the sunflower oil in a frying pan. Add the onion and carrot and cook over a medium heat, stirring, for about 5–7 minutes until the carrot is meltingly soft and is about to start caramelizing. This is a distinctively Ukrainian soffritto technique called *smazhennya* or *zazharka*.

4 Add the red pepper and tomato purée to the onion and carrot and cook it out for 2 minutes, then add the grated fresh tomato or fermented tomatoes, stir and reduce slightly before adding all of this to the broth.

5 Finally, add the shredded cabbage and beans to the broth and cook for about 7 minutes until cooked through.

6 Serve with a dollop of soured cream, chopped dill and *Pampushky*.

Come the spring, we pick basketfuls of sorrel from Mum's vegetable patch, collect duck eggs from her ducks and cook this emerald-green beauty. You can use chicken or vegetable stock, but rich duck stock tamed by sharp fresh sorrel is a winner for me. It's not a true *borshch* but more of a sorrel broth. Grandma Lusia always made a huge pile of *Frumentaty* (Moldovan flatbreads, *see* page 49) to go with this. I would recommend keeping the duck breasts for a different dish (use them instead of pork in the *Nudli* on page 98) and just using the back, legs, wings and giblets for this soup.

Зелений борщ | *Zelenyy borshch*
Sorrel broth

Serves 4–6

1 small onion, finely chopped
1 carrot, peeled and grated
2 potatoes, peeled and roughly chopped
100g (3½oz) beetroot leaves and stalks, chopped, or 1 small beetroot, peeled and cut into matchsticks
50g (2oz) sorrel, sliced with its stalks
2 spring onions, sliced

Stock
back, wings, legs and giblets (except the liver) of 1 medium duck
1 onion, peeled but kept whole
1 bay leaf
2.5 litres (4 pints) cold water
sea salt flakes and freshly ground black pepper

To serve
2 chicken's eggs (or duck eggs), hard-boiled, shelled and chopped
½ bunch of dill, chopped
½ bunch of parsley, chopped
Frumentaty (see page 49)

1 To make the stock, place the duck pieces and giblets, whole onion and bay leaf in a large saucepan, then cover with the measurement water and add a pinch of sea salt flakes. Bring to a simmer and skim the surface, discarding all the scum. Simmer on the lowest heat possible for 1½–2 hours or until the duck meat falls off the bone. The liquid will reduce by almost half. Keep skimming it from time to time.

2 Strain the stock into a large bowl, reserving the duck bits, but discarding the onion and bay leaf. Pour the liquid back into the pan. Check the seasoning and add salt and pepper to taste.

3 Pull the duck meat off the bones, discard the bones and set the meat aside.

4 Skim half a ladleful of duck broth from the very top (you are aiming to skim the fat here) and pour it into a frying pan. Boil off the liquid for a minute until you are left with just duck fat. Add the onion and carrot to the pan and sweat over a medium heat, stirring all the time, for about 5–7 minutes until they are soft and caramelized ever so slightly. These will bring beautiful sweetness to the broth.

5 Introduce the onion and carrot to your stock, followed by the potatoes, and cook for 10 minutes.

6 Add the beetroot leaves and stalks or beetroot matchsticks and cook for 5 minutes, then switch the heat off.

7 Place some duck meat in each serving bowl. Then place the raw, chopped sorrel and spring onions on top and pour the hot stock over them. Garnish with the chopped egg, dill and parsley, and serve with *Frumentaty*.

This is simply the best hangover cure there is. The meat needs to have a good amount of fat on it as this is the whole point of using gherkins – they cut through the fat. You should only use brined or fermented gherkins, as even the nicest vinegar will spoil this dish. Look for a label with 'ogórek kwaszony' in Polish or Eastern European shops (*see* page 152). Make the stock in advance and freeze it; it doesn't take long to make this soup once the stock is ready. The fat, salt and sugar from caramelized carrot will make you feel alive again.

Рассольник | *Rassol'nyk*
Gherkin, beef & barley broth

Serves 4

Stock

500g (1lb) pork ribs or beef short ribs
2.5L (4 pints) cold water
1 onion, peeled but kept whole
1 bay leaf
5 black peppercorns
5 allspice berries
100g (3½oz) pearl barley or rice

1 onion, diced 2 tablespoons sunflower oil
1 carrot, peeled and grated
20g (¾/¾oz) parsley root, peeled and finely chopped, or parsley stalks, finely chopped
100g (3½oz) gherkins, peeled and grated
200ml (7fl oz) gherkin brine from the jar
2 spring onions, finely chopped, to serve

1 To make the stock, cut the ribs into individual ribs, place in a large saucepan and cover with the water. Add the whole onion, bay leaf, peppercorns and allspice and bring to the boil.

2 Reduce the heat as soon as the water boils and skim the scum that rises to the surface. Simmer for a couple of hours while you watch your favourite TV series and eat leftover gherkins.

3 When the meat is tender and falling off the bone, add the pearl barley or rice and cook for 15 minutes until it is cooked, but still has a bite.

4 Meanwhile, sweat the diced onion in the sunflower oil in a frying pan over a medium heat for 5 minutes, then add the parsley root or stalks and carrot and continue to cook over a medium-low heat, stirring often, for 15 minutes or until everything is soft and starting to caramelize slightly. Add to the stock.

5 Add the gherkins to the stock, taste and add 100ml (3½fl oz) of the gherkin brine. Taste it and add more if you think it needs more salt. The broth should taste rich, but also a little salty, sweet and sour. Scatter with spring onions and serve with a huge hunk of good bread.

This is incredibly refreshing in the summer. I guess it's a hybrid of something that Russians call *okroshka* (which comes from *kroshit*, meaning 'to chop into small pieces') and the Ukrainian *kholodnyk* ('the cold one'). I like the idea of brining the beetroot first. And I like the idea of fresh radishes and cucumber in it, too. Add a small splash of sherry vinegar, and a tiny bit of Tabasco if you can't find fresh horseradish, to funk it up a little.

Холодник | *Kholodnyk*
Cold beetroot soup

Serves 6

500g (1lb) beetroot, peeled and halved
1.5 litres (2½ pints) cold water
1½ tablespoons sea salt flakes
½ tablespoon sugar or clear honey
1 litre (1¾pints) vegetable stock
1 waxy potato, peeled and diced
20g (¾oz) fresh horseradish, peeled and grated
freshly ground black pepper
ice cubes, to serve

To serve

100g (3½oz) radishes, finely chopped
½ cucumber, diced
4 spring onions, finely sliced
1 tablespoon chopped dill

1 Place the beetroot in a bowl or container, cover with the water and add the sea salt flakes and the sugar or honey. Leave it in your kitchen at room temperature for 2 days to let it brine lightly.

2 Drain the beetroot, reserving the brine. Cut it into thin slices and then into 5mm (¼ inch) dice.

3 Place the beetroot, stock and 300ml (½ pint) of the reserved brine in a saucepan, taste for seasoning, then bring to the boil.

4 Add the potato and cook for 15 minutes or until cooked through. Let the broth cool, then cover and chill in the refrigerator.

5 Add the horseradish just before serving (it is so volatile, it will make you cry but will dissipate into thin air quite rapidly). Serve the soup chilled, with an ice cube or two added, and garnished with the radishes, cucumber, spring onions and dill.

One of my first food memories is of my mother cooking this broth. My dad brought some dried ceps from Belarus, and I remember the intoxicating smell and how dark the broth was – it was almost black. My mum made it with homemade noodles, but I like to mix it up a bit and buckwheat gives it a lovely texture.

Mushroom broth with buckwheat

Serves 4

2 large potatoes, peeled and diced
100g (3½oz) buckwheat
1½ tablespoons sunflower oil
1 onion, chopped
1 carrot, peeled and grated
20g (¾oz) butter
50g (2oz) wild mushrooms, trimmed and sliced
sea salt flakes and freshly ground black pepper

Stock

50g (2oz) dried ceps
1 onion, peeled but kept whole
1 bay leaf
2.5 litres (4 pints) cold water

To serve
2 tablespoons chopped dill
50ml (2fl oz) soured cream
toasted rye bread

1 To make the stock, soak the ceps in cold water to cover for about 1 hour (this helps get rid of the grit), then strain through a fine sieve, reserving the liquid.

2 Place the ceps and their soaking liquid, whole onion and bay leaf in a saucepan and cover with the water. Bring to the boil and simmer for 15 minutes.

3 Season to taste with salt and pepper, add the potatoes and buckwheat, then cook for a further 15 minutes.

4 Meanwhile, put 1 tablespoon of the sunflower oil in a frying pan and sweat the chopped onion over a medium-low heat for 5 minutes. Add the carrot and cook for another 5 minutes, stirring often.

5 Add the carrot and onion to the broth, but don't rinse out the frying pan. Melt the butter in the pan over a medium-high heat and add the remaining sunflower oil. Fry the wild mushrooms for about 5–7 minutes until golden, then add them to the broth.

6 Serve the soup with the dill, soured cream and a piece of toasted rye bread.

This is *Rassol'nyk's* (*see* page 16) nouveau riche brother. The concept is similar – rich meaty broth and a sour element to cut right through the richness. But the addition of such decadent items as salami, olives and lemon take it to a whole new level. It should be rich, spicy and a little bit crazy-tasting. My grandmother used to make it with ox heart – boiled with some beef bones and then chopped into small pieces. Instead of the more traditional salami, I sometimes like to use diced and fried spicy cooking chorizo. Needless to say, if you have no time to make stock, just use the good stuff from your local butcher and the broth will then be ready in a matter of minutes.

Солянка | *Solyanka*
Piquant Russian broth

Serves 4

250g (8oz) good-quality salami,
  roughly chopped
3 tablespoons sunflower oil
1 onion, diced
1 tablespoon tomato purée
1 carrot, peeled and grated
1 teaspoon sugar
100g (3½oz) button mushrooms,
  trimmed and sliced
3 gherkins, grated
about 100ml (3½fl oz) gherkin brine
  from the jar
15 mixed pitted olives, sliced
10g (⅓oz) good-quality capers

Stock

1kg (2lb) beef bones
2.5 litres (4 pints) cold water
1 onion, peeled but kept whole
1 bay leaf
10 black peppercorns
5 allspice berries

To serve

½ lemon, halved and thinly sliced
1 tablespoon chopped parsley

1 To make the stock, place the beef bones in a large saucepan and cover with the measurement water. Add the whole onion, bay leaf, peppercorns and allspice berries and bring to the boil. Lower the heat as soon as the water boils and skim off the scum that rises to the surface. Cook for 1½ hours – the broth should reduce a little and smell strongly of beef.

2 Add the salami pieces to the stock.

3 Heat 2 tablespoons of the sunflower oil in a frying pan and sweat the diced onion for 5 minutes. Add the tomato purée, carrot and sugar and cook for another 5 minutes, stirring often.

4 Place the carrot mixture in the broth and wipe out the frying pan. Heat the remaining tablespoon of oil in the pan and fry the mushrooms until they turn golden. Add them to the broth along with the gherkins and some of the gherkin brine. Taste it and add some more if you think it needs it.

5 Finally, add the olives and capers and cook for another 2 minutes.

6 Serve the *solyanka* with the lemon slices and chopped parsley.

This is Ukrainian penicillin. My mum would always use an old boiling chicken, which can be a little tough, yes, but the flavour is incomparable. She would always make this if we were ill. Even though there is no scientific proof that chicken soup actually helps you get better, the love that comes with it definitely has a positive impact. The dumplings are simple, and it's all a little stark, but the flavour is so pure. Give this a go, especially when your loved one is ill or when it's cold and drizzly outside.

Chicken broth with dumplings

Serves 4

1 boiling chicken, jointed
   into 8 pieces
2.5 litres (4 pints) cold
   water
1 bay leaf
1 onion, peeled but
   kept whole
1 carrot, peeled and
   thinly sliced
sea salt flakes and freshly
   ground black pepper

Dumplings

1 large egg
50ml (2fl oz) cold water
½ teaspoon fine sea salt
125g (4oz) plain flour

To serve

1 spring onion,
   thinly sliced
2 tablespoons chopped dill
crusty sourdough bread

1 Place the chicken pieces in a large saucepan and cover with the water. Add the bay leaf, whole onion and seasoning, and bring to the boil. Skim off the scum and leave to simmer over a very low heat for 1 hour, or 1½ hours if using a boiling chicken, until cooked through.

2 To make the dumpling mixture, beat the egg lightly in a bowl, then add the measurement water and salt and gradually sift in the flour. Work into a paste.

3 Add the carrot to the stock, then drop in separate teaspoonfuls of the dumpling paste and boil for 5 minutes.

4 Serve with the spring onion, dill and a big hunk of crusty sourdough bread for dipping.

Plum fruit leather, called *tklapi*, is normally used in Georgia to add a sensuous sour note to this soup, but in Ukraine we usually just use tomato. I like to add some pomegranate molasses, too, for that extra sweet-and-sour kick. This thick, sumptuous soup is another incredible hangover cure.

Харчо | *Kharcho*
Spicy Georgian beef soup

Serves 4

2 dried red chillies, crushed
  (keep the seeds)
pinch of saffron threads
1 carrot, peeled and diced
100g (3½oz) white long-grain rice
1 beef tomato (skin discarded), grated
2 tablespoons pomegranate molasses
4 small garlic cloves, peeled
100g (3½oz) walnuts, toasted
sea salt flakes and freshly ground
  black pepper

Stock
600g (1lb 3oz) Jacob's ladder (beef
  short ribs, cut into individual ribs)
  or beef shin
2 tablespoons sunflower oil
3 litres (5¼ pints) cold water
2 onions, thinly sliced
1 bay leaf
5 black peppercorns
1 teaspoon coriander seeds, toasted
  and crushed

To serve
2 tablespoons chopped fresh coriander
2 tablespoons chopped purple
  (or regular) basil

1 To make the stock, first season the ribs or shin well with salt and pepper. Heat the sunflower oil in a large saucepan and brown the meat. Cover with the water and bring to the boil, then lower the heat and simmer for 1 hour.

2 Add the onions, bay leaf, peppercorns and crushed coriander seeds and cook for another 30–60 minutes. You want the meat to start falling apart.

3 Once the beef is tender, add the crushed chillies, saffron, carrot and rice to the stock and cook for 10 minutes.

4 Add the grated tomato and pomegranate molasses and cook for another 10 minutes. Taste and season the soup – it should be spicy and sharp.

5 Bash the garlic cloves with a pinch of sea salt flakes using a pestle and mortar, then add the walnuts and bash until it turns into a paste. Add to the broth and cook for another 5 minutes. The soup should be thick and luscious. Serve it with the fresh coriander and basil.

The word *tuzluk* is normally used in the Caucasus region to describe a brine for salting fish or meat. However, in the south of Ukraine *tuzluk* is what we call a simple mutton broth served with seasoned raw onions. We always used to make it when camping by the Dnieper River, cooked over a campfire in a cauldron for a few hours while the fathers fished, mothers chatted and chopped salads, and the kids swam in the river. I always associate this broth with a sense of adventure. Once, when I was five, we went camping with my huge extended family. It was a beautiful July afternoon when a huge storm came out of nowhere. Luckily, my uncle had an old Volga truck in which all 15 of us huddled up and sipped on *tuzluk* that we had managed to save, listening to the banging of torn willow branches against the roof of the car.

Тузлук | *Tuzluk*

Campfire mutton broth

Serves 6–8

1.5kg (3lb) mutton or lamb ribs,
   cut into individual ribs
3.5 litres (5½ pints) cold water
3 small onions, peeled but kept whole
6 small potatoes, peeled but kept whole
2 bay leaves
sea salt flakes and freshly ground
   black pepper

To serve

2 small red onions, thinly sliced
1 bunch of parsley, chopped
1 bunch of dill, chopped
1 bunch of fresh coriander, chopped

1 Place the mutton or lamb ribs in a large saucepan and cover with the water. Season with salt and pepper and bring to the boil. Skim off the scum and add the whole onions. Simmer for 2 hours or until the meat starts falling off the bone.

2 Add the whole peeled potatoes and simmer for 20 minutes or until the potatoes are cooked but not falling apart. Keep skimming off any scum that rises to the surface.

3 When the broth is ready, place the sliced raw red onions in a bowl, season well with salt and give them a quick massage. Then add a ladleful of the hot broth to kill any raw onion harshness. Take out the meat and potatoes and place them on a platter. Everybody serves themselves broth and takes a little bit of meat, some potatoes and the broth-soaked raw onions. Sprinkle over the chopped herbs and eat outside at dusk, preferably by a campfire.

I visited Baku when I was two years old. My parents were really brave to take me together with my 10-year-old brother on a 1,300-mile road trip in our old Zhiguli. It took us two days and finally we were there, just south of Iran, by the Caspian Sea. I wish I remembered more of the trip. All I have is a photo of my brother and me in a meadow by a lake, and a vague memory of watching TV in Azerbaijan. Even though nobody believes me, I remember Gorbachev talking passionately about something (*perestroika*?) on TV and how serious my parents' faces looked. This soup is traditionally cooked in individual clay serving pots, but I prefer cooking it in a large pot and then decanting it into small bowls.

Піті | Piti
Azerbaijani chickpea & mutton soup

Serves 6

600g (1lb 3oz) mutton or lamb neck, cut into 6 large pieces
1 onion, peeled but kept whole
2 dried limes, pierced
2.5 litres (4 pints) cold water
125g (4oz) dried chickpeas, soaked in cold water overnight and drained, or 400g (13oz) can chickpeas, drained and rinsed
6 new potatoes, peeled but kept whole
1 bunch of parsley, stalks only
½ teaspoon saffron threads
1 teaspoon cumin seeds
sea salt flakes and freshly ground black pepper

To serve
½ bunch of fresh coriander
½ bunch of dill

1 Place the meat, whole onion and dried limes in a large saucepan and cover with the water. Cook over a low heat for 1 hour or until the meat is tender.

2 Add the chickpeas, potatoes, parsley stalks and the spices, and simmer for another hour or until the meat is meltingly tender and the chickpeas and potatoes are cooked. Season the broth well.

3 Take the potatoes and lamb out and serve them separately on the table, for people to take what they want themselves. Place the half-bunches of herbs on the table and again let your guests pinch off whatever leaves they want.

This, like all the other Armenian recipes in this book, is Aunt Nina's recipe. When she first sent it through, she said, 'If you can, use Alycha prunes; if not, just regular prunes – not the smoked variety!' I would actually love to get my hands on some smoked prunes – how ace do they sound? Nina normally just drops a couple of prunes into the broth while cooking the chickpeas, but I like to add some pomegranate molasses. Do whatever is easier or suits your tastes, as both versions are good.

Кюфта | *Kyufta*
Armenian soup with lamb & prune meatballs

Serves 4

2 litres (3½ pints) meat
 or vegetable stock
½ cinnamon stick
125g (4oz) dried chickpeas,
 soaked overnight in
 cold water and drained,
 or 400g (13oz) can
 chickpeas, drained and
 well rinsed
2 tablespoons pomegranate
 molasses
1 tablespoon brown sugar
 (optional)
300g (10oz) minced lamb
1 small onion, grated
2 tablespoons (uncooked)
 white long-grain rice
6 pitted prunes, halved
sea salt flakes and freshly
 ground black pepper

To serve
½ bunch of dill, finely
 chopped
½ bunch of fresh coriander,
 finely chopped

1 Place the stock and cinnamon stick in a saucepan, add the chickpeas and bring to the boil. Stir in the pomegranate molasses, and the sugar, if the broth seems a little too sour. Reduce the heat and simmer – if using soaked chickpeas, simmer for 55 minutes, or 5 minutes for canned – until the chickpeas are cooked through, but still have a crisp texture. Season the broth with salt and pepper once the chickpeas are cooked.

2 Meanwhile, make the meatballs. Place the lamb, onion and uncooked rice in a bowl, season well and give it all a really good mix with your hands.

3 Wash your hands, but do not dry them, as it is easier to shape the *kyufta* with wet hands. Roll the mixture into 12 oblong meatballs, stuffing a prune half in the middle of each.

4 Drop the *kyufta* into the broth and cook for 20–25 minutes or until the rice in the *kyufta* is tender and the meat is cooked through. Taste the broth – it should be well seasoned and slightly sweet and sour. Serve with the chopped herbs.

This is my half-Armenian Aunt Nina's favourite family dish. When she was little, she used to spend every summer at her Armenian grandparents' *dacha* in Karabakh, a predominantly Armenian territory in Azerbaijan. She was the eldest of all her cousins, so she was the one helping in the kitchen. She still remembers laboriously stirring this soup, which took hours to make, as all they had back in the 1950s was a kerosene stove.

Танов | *Tanov*

Armenian cold yogurt & sorrel soup

Serves 4

400ml (14fl oz) natural yogurt
1 litre (1¾ pints) water
1 egg, lightly beaten
100g (3½oz) white long-grain rice
100g (3½oz) spinach, chopped
50g (2oz) sorrel, chopped
½ bunch of fresh coriander, chopped
½ bunch of dill, chopped
sea salt flakes and freshly ground black pepper

1 Mix the yogurt, water and egg together in a bowl. Season this well and give it a good whisk to incorporate the egg thoroughly.

2 Place the rice in a large saucepan, cover with the yogurt mixture and bring to the boil, stirring constantly to prevent the egg and yogurt curdling.

3 Cook over a low heat, stirring constantly, for about 10 minutes or until the rice is cooked.

4 Add the spinach, sorrel and the herbs and cook for another minute. Remove from the heat and let it cool in the refrigerator, then serve cold.

They sometimes pop a glowing ember into this broth in Russia to make sure that it smells extra smoky (this dish is often cooked over a campfire), which is a bit extreme – but Russians can be a little extreme sometimes, eh? If you can't find crayfish, use large prawns or langoustines with their shells on. It may not be particularly authentic, but I'm sure a tsar wouldn't have minded. London is apparently being plagued by alien American crayfish, so if you live in the UK anywhere near the capital, give my hero Crayfish Bob a ring, who will gladly catch them and sell them to you. They are cheap and beat any farmed prawns hands down.

Царська юшка | *Tsarska yushka*

Tsar's surf & turf

Serves 5–6

1 chicken carcass
  or 10 chicken wings
1 small onion, peeled,
  but kept whole
2 carrots, peeled and
  roughly chopped
1 parsley root or a
  handful of parsley
  stalks, chopped
10 black peppercorns
2.5 litres (4 pints) cold
  water
1 whole sea bass or trout,
  gutted and scaled
10 raw crayfish or large
  prawns or langoustines,
  shells and heads on
1 bunch of dill, stalks only
100g (3½oz) button
  mushrooms, trimmed
  and chopped

To serve
1 lemon, halved and
  thinly sliced
2 tablespoons chopped
  parsley

1 Place the chicken carcass or wings, whole onion, carrots, parsley root or stalks and peppercorns in a large saucepan and cover with the water. Bring to the boil, then lower the heat and simmer, skimming off the scum from time to time, for 1 hour. Remove the carcass or wings and discard.

2 Cut the head and tail off the fish and pop those into the broth (reserve the body), then add the shellfish and dill stalks and simmer for 5 minutes.

3 Cut across the fish body (bones and all) into 6 steaks and pop them into the broth. Add the mushrooms and cook for another 5 minutes until the shellfish is pink and the fish cooked through. Serve with a slice of lemon and the chopped parsley.

Хлібні вироби
Breads & Pastries

The word *pampushka* can be used to describe a gorgeous plump woman and is one of my favourite words. Pam-poo-shka! These *pampushky* are traditionally served with red *borshch* (*see* page 12). In Ukraine, we would use regular garlic, so if you can't find wet (new) garlic don't worry – it will still be delicious.

Пампушки | *Pampushky*

Ukrainian garlic bread

Makes 8 breads

15g (½oz) fresh yeast or 7g (¼oz) dried active yeast
1 teaspoon caster sugar
225ml (7½fl oz) warm water
400g (13oz) strong white flour, plus extra for dusting
8g (⅓oz) fine sea salt
3 tablespoons sunflower oil, plus extra for oiling
20g (¾oz) wet (new) or regular garlic, crushed
½ bunch of parsley, finely chopped
1 duck (or chicken) egg, beaten, to glaze

1 First make a 'sponge', which is a type of yeasty starter. Dissolve the yeast and sugar in the measurement water (make sure it's blood temperature – hot water would kill the yeast!). Add 200g (7oz) of the flour and mix roughly. Cover with clingfilm and leave to prove in the refrigerator overnight.

2 The next morning, add the rest of the flour and fine sea salt to the starter and knead on a well-floured work surface until the dough is smooth and comes away from your hands easily.

3 Divide the dough into 8 pieces and shape into round buns. Put them side by side in an oiled round ovenproof dish or a 24cm (9½ inch) round cake tin, cover and let them prove again, this time in a warm place, until doubled in size. They will join together just like hot cross buns do.

4 Meanwhile, preheat the oven to 220°C/425°F/Gas Mark 7. To make the basting oil, simply stir the crushed garlic through the oil with a small pinch of sea salt and the parsley, then let it infuse.

5 When the *pampushky* look plump and ready, brush them generously with some beaten egg to glaze and bake for 20–25 minutes or until they form a glistening golden crust. Take them out and baste them with the garlic oil. Serve immediately.

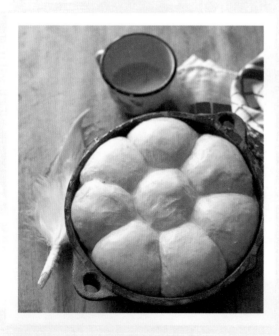

There were Greek communities in Crimea for many centuries, but most of them were relocated to the Ukrainian northern shores of the Sea of Azov under Catherine the Great, who annexed Crimea from the Ottoman Empire in 1783. A Greek friend of ours from one such community taught us how to make this. We would normally use salted *Syr* here (*see* page 109), but feta works just fine. I sometimes add chopped herbs, such as dill, parsley, coriander or basil, for an extra boost of flavour.

Плакопси | *Plakopsy*
Greek breads with spring onions

Makes 4

200ml (7fl oz) cold water
1 egg, lightly beaten
450g (14½oz) plain flour, plus extra for dusting
400g (13oz) feta cheese, crumbled
10 spring onions, roughly chopped
50ml (2fl oz) sunflower oil, plus extra for brushing
sea salt flakes

1 Mix the water, egg and a pinch of salt together in a large bowl. Gradually add the flour, mixing it in with a fork first and then with your hands.

2 Flour your work surface really well and knead the dough until it stops sticking to your hands.

3 Mix the feta with the spring onions. Taste and add salt only if needed. Divide the filling into 4 portions.

4 Divide the dough into 4 pieces. Flour the work surface well and roll one piece of dough out as thinly as you can into a 30cm (12 inch) circle. Moisten the top of the sheet with a little sunflower oil. Take one-quarter of the filling and spread most of it over the rolled-out dough, leaving about a 5cm (2 inch) border. Then fold 2 opposite sides of the dough inwards to overlap, brush with a little more oil and sprinkle over the remaining filling, then fold the other 2 sides over to form a square. Flour and lightly roll over the folded bread, then set aside.

5 Repeat with the rest of the dough pieces and filling.

6 Heat the 50ml (2fl oz) sunflower oil in a large frying pan and fry the breads, one at a time, for 3 minutes on each side, lowering the heat if you see them catching a bit.

7 Let the breads cool for a minute and then eat with some *kefir* (*see* page 8) or *ayran* (a salty yogurt drink).

These breads are traditionally shallow-fried, but if you like to be healthier, simply brush the breads with sunflower oil or butter and pop them under the grill for 3 minutes on each side. You can also use raw egg instead of cheese – simply mix two eggs with all of the herbs.

Плачінди з щавелем | *Plachindy z shchavelem*

Moldovan breads with cheese & sorrel

Makes 4

1 x recipe quantity *Kefir* Dough
  (*see* page 48)
plain flour, for dusting
50ml (2fl oz) sunflower oil

Filling

400g (13oz) feta cheese, crumbled
50g (2oz) sorrel or fresh spinach leaves,
  finely chopped
4 spring onions, finely chopped
2 tablespoons chopped dill
4 scant tablespoons sunflower oil

1 Divide the *Kefir* dough into 4 pieces. Flour the work surface really well and roll out each piece of dough, one by one, into a 20cm (8 inch) diameter circle.

3 For the filling, mix the feta, sorrel or spinach, spring onions and dill together, making sure that the feta is finely crumbled.

4 Moisten the surface of one dough circle with 1 scant tablespoon of the sunflower oil and sprinkle one-quarter of the filling over the whole surface.

5 Next, take one edge of the circle and fold it into the middle. Now bring the edge of the first fold into the middle and fold again. Repeat until you have created about 7 folds (fewer won't seal the filling in properly). The dough should resemble a flattened moneybag.

6 Make sure all the edges are firmly pinched together in the middle of the flatbread, flour the top lightly and gently flatten the moneybag with your rolling pin.

7 Repeat with the remaining dough circles and filling.

8 Heat the 50ml (2fl oz) sunflower oil in a frying pan until hot and gently lower in each flatbread, one at a time. The first one will take about 3 minutes on each side, but as the oil heats up, the next ones will take about 2–2½ minutes on each side. You can alternatively brush them with oil and cook them under your grill. The result will be somewhat different but still delicious.

It was really hard to write this recipe, as my grandmother always said to add as much flour as the liquid would take. Go by your instinct – if the dough is too wet, add a little more flour than my recipe specifies. You will also incorporate more flour when you knead the dough. My grandmother often used the whey that was left over from making cheese (*see Syr,* page 109) instead of *kefir* (*see* page 8) for this, but you can also use natural yogurt let down with a little water.

Kefir dough

Makes about 600g (1lb 3oz) dough

250g (8oz) *kefir*
½ tablespoon sunflower oil
½ tablespoon white wine vinegar
½ tablespoon granulated sugar
½ teaspoon salt
350g (11½oz) plain flour, plus extra for dusting
1 scant teaspoon bicarbonate of soda

1 Place the *kefir*, sunflower oil, vinegar, sugar and salt in a large bowl and mix together well with a fork.

2 Sift the flour with the bicarbonate of soda, then sift again into the *kefir* mixture and mix in. The dough should be soft and pillowy. If it's still slightly sticky, heavily flour your work surface and start kneading the dough, incorporating more flour into it. The dough should stop sticking to your hands when it's ready but also remain soft.

I have had trouble finding the name for these in my research, but this is what my grandmother called this lazy version of Moldovan *plachindy* (*see* page 47). *Frumentaty* may have come from a dialect – no one is sure and we didn't think to ask my grandma when she was still with us. I say 'lazy' *plachindy* because instead of filling the dough she simply mixed the filling into it. Also, instead of *kefir* she would always use whey to make these. You can always use watered-down natural yogurt instead.

Фрументати | *Frumentaty*
Moldovan lazy flatbreads

Makes 6

150ml (¼ pint) *kefir* or
   whey (*see* page 109)
50ml (2fl oz) sunflower
   oil, plus ¼ tablespoon
¼ tablespoon white wine
   vinegar
¼ tablespoon sugar
¼ teaspoon fine sea salt
200g (7oz) feta cheese,
   crumbled
4 spring onions,
   finely sliced
½ small bunch of dill,
   chopped
350g (11½oz) plain flour,
   plus an extra 100g
   (3½oz) for dusting
1 scant teaspoon
   bicarbonate of soda

1 Mix the kefir or whey, the ¼ tablespoon of sunflower oil, vinegar, sugar and salt together in a large bowl. Add the feta, spring onions and dill and mix in well with a fork.

2 Sift the flour with the bicarbonate of soda, then sift again into the kefir or whey mixture and mix in.

3 The dough should be soft and pillowy. If it's still a bit sticky, heavily flour your work surface and start kneading the dough and incorporating more flour. The dough will remain very slightly sticky from all the cheese.

4 Divide the dough into 6 pieces. Flour your work surface really well and roll each one out into a 15cm (6-inch) diameter circle.

5 Heat the 50ml (2fl oz) sunflower oil in a large frying pan and fry the breads, one at a time, for 3 minutes on each side, lowering the heat if you see them catching. Alternatively, brush the breads with oil or butter and cook them under your grill.

There are many versions of this dish including sweet ones, and Moldovan friends tell me that their grannies call this dish *invirtita* and *saralie*. My half-Moldovan grandmothers used to make this all the time and it's hard to stop eating it – the pastry is crispy on the outside and soft and salty on the inside. There is also a version using goose or duck scratchings instead of cheese that is equally glorious, but pieces of crispy streaky bacon would work equally well. Don't be scared of this dish – you should attempt it when in a playful mood. The pastry will start stretching slowly and then it can suddenly go nuts, so have fun with it, embrace the holes and stop stretching just in time before it tears completely.

Вертута | *Vertuta*
Moldovan giant cheese twist

Serves 8

2 eggs, lightly beaten
175ml (6fl oz) warm water
360g (11¾oz) plain flour,
   plus extra for dusting
4 tablespoons sunflower
   oil, plus extra for oiling
400g (13oz) salted *Syr* (*see*
   page 109) or feta cheese,
   crumbled

1 Mix 1 of the eggs and the measurement water together in a large bowl. Gradually add the flour, stirring the mixture well with a fork and working it into a slightly sticky pastry dough.

2 Cover the dough with clingfilm and leave to rest in the refrigerator for at least 30 minutes, preferably 1 hour. It should be firm and only slightly wet.

3 Flour the work surface really well and knead the dough briefly until it stops sticking to your hands. If the dough feels soft and very sticky, then add more flour to your work surface and knead it into the dough.

4 Divide the dough into 2 pieces. Roll one piece into a 30cm (12 inch) diameter circle. Gently stretch the edges of the circle with your hands.

5 Flour your work surface very, very heavily – you will later place your stretched pastry on it and it will have to be very well floured so that you can roll it up.

6 Preheat the oven to 200°C/400°F/Gas Mark 6.

7 Now lift the pastry circle and (gently!) suspend the edge over the back of your hands. Keep spinning it, moving your knuckles gently around. The weight of

the pastry at the bottom will help stretch the thicker edges of the pastry over your knuckles. Holes will probably appear, but don't worry – a couple are fine. The trick is to be confident when handling the dough. If you can see that a particular area needs stretching, then move your hands round to it; don't feel you have to stick to manipulating the edges. Just watch that it doesn't break completely, so stop immediately if you feel that it's about to collapse.

8 The dough should stretch to about 60–80cm (23½–31½ inches) in diameter and ideally, as my mum says, you should be able to read a newspaper through it. Carefully place it on your well-floured work surface. If the edges are still a lot thicker than the middle, stretch them gently.

9 Carefully brush 2 tablespoons of the sunflower oil all over the pastry – my grandmother used sterilized goose feathers to do this. Then sprinkle over half the cheese.

10 Next, roll out the second piece of dough and stretch it like you did the first one, again into a thin sheet about 60–80cm (23½–31½ inches) in diameter. Gently place it over the first sheet. Oil the top of it as before and sprinkle over the remaining cheese.

11 Starting at the edge nearest to you, roll both sheets of pastry up together into a long sausage, keeping it an even size all the way along; if the middle becomes too thick, try to roll it out to the edges. Cut off any extra dough that doesn't have cheese to avoid the twist getting too fat. Twist it at either end as if you are gently wringing a piece of clothing. If you feel that both ends are too thick and don't have enough cheese in them, just cut them off!

12 Finally, keep one end still and curl the other around it, creating a beautiful shell shape (think ammonite fossils).

13 Brush the *vertuta* very generously with the remaining beaten egg. I simply tip the whole beaten egg on and rub it over the *vertuta* gently with my hands. Oil a baking sheet or a large, shallow cake tin lightly, pop the *vertuta* on and bake it for 40 minutes or until golden brown all over. Let it cool slightly and eat half of it at one sitting.

These are basically the most incredible stuffed savoury doughnuts. We often went to Genichesk by the Sea of Azov, the shallowest sea in the world. You had to walk for at least 300m (428 yards) until the water started reaching your knees... a five-year-old's knees at that! While we were busy walking for miles trying to get sufficiently wet, my mum and Aunt Zhenia would be frying mountains of *pyrizhky* with every filling imaginable. I have included three of my favourite fillings here, egg and spring onion, potato, and hearts and livers as I love offal – chicken gizzards have always been one of my favourite things to eat. Hearts add great texture and the livers add flavour. We would run back to the tiny beach hut, sandy and ravenous, get our bodies covered in *kefir* (there was no sunscreen back then, so that was the sunburn remedy) and devour loads of these with a light soup. There was also more than one sweet version. Sliced fresh ripe apricots and sour cherries have always made the most delectable of fillings.

Пиріжки | *Pyrizhky*
Ukrainian stuffed buns

Milk & yeast dough
Makes about 600g
(1lb 3oz)

½ tablespoon sunflower oil
250ml (8fl oz) milk at room temperature
10g (⅓oz) fresh yeast or 7g (¼oz) dry yeast
½ tablespoon granulated sugar
½ teaspoon salt
350–400g (11½–13oz) plain flour, plus extra for dusting
about 100ml (3½fl oz) sunflower oil

1 First make the dough: whisk the oil, milk, yeast, sugar and salt together with a fork in a bowl for a minute to incorporate some air into the liquid.

2 Sift the flour, then gradually add it to the liquid and work it into a soft, pillowy dough in the bowl. Add enough flour to make it doughy – it may still be a little damp, but don't worry, as you can incorporate more flour when you knead it later. Cover the bowl with clingfilm and leave to prove in a warm place for 45 minutes or until the dough has doubled in size.

3 Knead the dough on a well-floured work surface. It should be pleasantly soft but should not stick to your hands. Divide the dough into 8–10 pieces (about 80–60g/3–2¼oz each) depending which filling you are using.

4 Next make your chosen filling.

Egg & spring onion filling *Pyrizhky z yaytsem* (makes 8)

3 eggs, hard-boiled, shelled and finely chopped
50g (2oz) spring onions, finely chopped
20g (³⁄₄oz) dill, stalks and all, finely chopped
sea salt flakes

Potato filling *Pyrizhky z kartopleyu* (makes 10)

300g (10oz) potatoes, peeled and chopped
50g (2oz) butter, melted
50ml (2fl oz) warm milk
1 tablespoon sunflower oil
100g (3½oz) shallots, diced
fine sea salt and freshly ground black pepper

Hearts & liver filling *Pyrizhky z liverom* (makes 10)

2 tablespoons sunflower oil
100g (3½oz) shallots, sliced
2 tablespoons Madeira
150g (5oz) chicken hearts
150g (5oz) chicken livers
sea salt flakes and freshly ground black pepper

For the egg and spring onion filling, mix the hard-boiled eggs with the spring onions and dill, and season to taste with salt.

For the potato filling, place the potatoes in a saucepan with cold water to cover, season well with salt and bring them to the boil. Cook for 15 minutes or until they can be easily pierced with a knife. Drain the potatoes and mash them finely with the butter and milk.

Heat the sunflower oil in a frying pan and fry the shallots for about 10 minutes or until they are soft and nicely caramelized, then mix them with the potato and check the seasoning.

For the hearts and liver filling, heat 1 tablespoon of the sunflower oil in a frying pan and cook the shallots over a medium-low heat for 10 minutes or until they start turning golden. Add the Madeira and deglaze the pan and let almost all the liquid boil off. Remove the shallots from the pan.

Heat the remaining tablespoon of oil and sauté the chicken hearts over a medium-high heat, stirring a few times, for 5 minutes until they start to caramelize. Add the livers to the pan, season well and sauté over a medium-high heat for another 5 minutes. Lower the heat, return the shallots to the pan and cover with a lid. Let it all steam for another 7 minutes, then let the mix cool in a bowl.

5 Flour the work surface really well and roll each piece of dough out into a 10cm (4 inch) diameter circle. Place about 25g (1oz) of your chosen filling in the centre of each dough circle. Bring the edges up and pinch them together to seal, then flip the buns seam side down (on the floured work surface) and gently flatten them with your hand.

6 Heat the sunflower oil in a large frying pan until very hot and fry the *pyrizhky*, 4–6 at a time depending on the size of your pan, for 3 minutes on each side or until golden all over, lowering the heat if you see them catching. Drain them on kitchen paper and serve immediately instead of bread with some lovely broth or as a snack on their own.

This is Crimean Tartar's national dish. When I was little we used to spend half the summer in Crimea with my Russian grandma Vera. People would carry *chebureky* – one of the most beautiful street food snacks – along the beach. The filling must be incredibly juicy, and originally Tartars would add some lard from a type of fat-rumped sheep. In Ukraine, we add a little bit of *kefir* to the filling instead. But don't be alarmed if the mixture looks really liquid – this is the way it should be – although be careful when you bite into them, as there will be a lot of juice. Meat provenance is important here, so make sure you use the best lamb possible. We normally use a mixture of minced pork neck and beef rump, but of course this is a blatant Ukrainization; Muslims would only use mutton or beef.

Чебуреки | *Chebureky*
Tartar lamb turnovers

Makes 6

Pastry dough
250ml (8fl oz) cold water
1 egg, lightly beaten
½ tablespoon sugar
½ teaspoon fine sea salt
½ tablespoon sunflower
 oil
500g (1lb) plain flour, plus
 extra for dusting

Filling
200g (7oz) minced lamb
100g (3½oz) onions,
 grated
1 tablespoon *kefir*
 (optional)
½ teaspoon fine sea salt
100ml (3½fl oz) sunflower
 oil

1 To make the pastry dough, place the measurement water in a large bowl and add the egg, sugar, salt and oil. Gradually add the flour and mix it into a firm dough.

2 Knead the dough on a floured work surface and then cover in clingfilm and chill in the refrigerator for at least 20 minutes.

3 For the filling, place the lamb, onions and *kefir*, if using, in a bowl, season with the salt and mix together really well, preferably with your hands.

4 Divide the dough into 6 pieces and roll out each piece on a floured work surface as thinly as you can, about 23cm (9 inches) in diameter. Place 2 full tablespoons of the mince mixture inside each dough circle and spread it thinly, leaving a 5cm (2 inch) border around the edge. Fip one side of the circles over the filling and pinch the edges firmly together to make large half-moon turnovers.

5 Heat the sunflower oil in a large frying pan and fry the *chebureky* one at a time over a medium-high heat for 3 minutes on each side, lowering the heat if you see them browning too fast. Eat immediately, but watch that you don't burn yourself!

These make ideal barbecue food, and this is my brother Sasha's signature barbecue recipe that he picked up at our local Armenian restaurant. If you can't find lavash flatbreads (Turkish and Persian ones are very similar to the Armenian ones), you can also use flour tortilla wraps. Suluguni is a stringy, salty cheese from Georgia; do give it a go if you can find it, as it is more stretchy and makes a nice change from the ubiquitous haloumi, which has a more crumbly texture.

Caucasian barbecue flatbreads

Makes 6

2 garlic cloves, crushed

200g (7oz) suluguni or haloumi cheese, roughly chopped

50g (2oz) fresh coriander, stalks and leaves

50g (2oz) parsley stalks and leaves

1½ lavash, about 30 x 50cm (12 x 20 inches) each, or 6 flour tortilla wraps

50g (2oz) butter, melted, or 50ml (2fl oz) sunflower oil

1 Place the garlic, cheese and herbs in a food processor and blitz them into a paste.

2 Cut the whole lavash into quarters, and cut the ½ lavash in half so you have 6 flatbreads. Divide the filling between each flatbread or tortilla and wrap them up into parcels.

3 Brush the parcels with the melted butter, then wrap them individually in foil, pop them on the barbecue and cook for about 10 minutes. The filling will melt inside. Alternatively, brush them with the sunflower oil and cook in a griddle pan over a high heat or under a preheated hot grill for 3 minutes on each side. Serve with the BBQ Catfish (see page 140).

Овочі та салати

Vegetables & Salads

This is when baba ganoush decided to invite his friends round to dance the *mamushka*. I love adding basil and fresh coriander to this (shock, horror, my dear Italian friends!) You have to make sure that the vegetables are properly charred, and doing this over a barbecue would be ideal, but the open flame of the hob or your grill would do the job just fine. Unrefined sunflower oil, powerful in smell and flavour as it is, may be a little bit like Marmite; try it – it's now widely available – and if you hate it, use rapeseed oil instead. It went out of favour among those who could afford the newly available olive oil in the early Noughties in Ukraine, but now it is enjoying a comeback.

Grilled vegetable 'caviar'

Serves 6 as a dip

2 beef tomatoes
2 long green peppers
1 aubergine
2 garlic cloves, crushed
½ small red onion, finely diced
½ tablespoon unrefined sunflower oil, plus extra for oiling (optional)
1 tablespoon chopped dill
1 tablespoon chopped parsley
1 tablespoon chopped fresh coriander
1 tablespoon chopped basil
sea salt flakes and freshly ground black pepper
crusty bread, to serve

1 Place the tomatoes, green peppers and aubergine on a barbecue or oil lightly and place under the grill. Cook them, turning occasionally, until the vegetables are well charred and have pretty much collapsed.

2 Pop the vegetables into a large bowl, cover with clingfilm and leave them to sweat for 10 minutes – it will then be easier to take the skins off.

3 Core and deseed the peppers, discarding the stalks. Take off most of the tomato and aubergine skins; if some black bits remain, don't worry, as they will add a beautiful smoky flavour. Roughly chop all the grilled vegetables.

4 Mix the chopped vegetables with the garlic and red onion, then dress with a slither of the oil. Season well with salt and pepper, then stir through the herbs. Serve with some crusty bread.

This is my version of a salad that my cousin Ira used to bring to our huge family gatherings. The original had a mayo dressing as far as I remember, and the beetroot was boiled. The dressing should be really garlicky; the edges of the beetroot crispy and intense. Spring onion would make a great substitute or an addition to fresh coriander.

Beetroot & prune salad

Serves 6 as a side

1kg (2lb) beetroot, peeled and each sliced into 8 wedges

2 tablespoons sunflower oil

100ml (3½fl oz) soured cream

1 tablespoon balsamic vinegar

2 garlic cloves, crushed

25g (1oz) good-quality pitted prunes, roughly chopped

25g (1oz) walnut halves, toasted and halved lengthways

2 tablespoons fresh coriander leaves

sea salt flakes and freshly ground black pepper

1 Preheat the oven to 200°C/400°F/Gas Mark 6. Toss the beetroot in the oil and season generously with salt and pepper. Place in a roasting tin and bake for 40 minutes or until the beetroot is tender and starts caramelizing at the edges.

2 Mix the soured cream, balsamic vinegar and garlic together, season well with salt and pepper and stir. Add a little bit of water if the dressing is too thick.

3 Serve the beetroot on a platter, drizzled with the dressing and topped with the prunes, walnuts and coriander.

Lobio simply means 'beans' in most of the Caucasus region, and there are thousands of recipes for them including soupy versions and crushed-bean versions. This is my interpretation of a dish documented by William Pokhlebkin, one of my favourite food writers – the Alan Davidson of Soviet food writing. Even though his books adhere to a dry technical style dictated by the state at the time, his love and admiration for the vast variety of Soviet cuisines manages to shine through and infect with gastronomic wanderlust.

Лобіо | *Lobio*
Georgian kidney bean salad

Serves 2

¼ teaspoon fenugreek
   seeds
1 teaspoon coriander seeds
1 teaspoon fennel seeds
3 tablespoons sunflower
   oil
1 small onion, sliced
400g (13oz) can red
   kidney beans, drained
   and rinsed
1 teaspoon sherry vinegar
½ teaspoon brown sugar
½ bunch of fresh
   coriander, chopped
2 sprigs of parsley,
   chopped
2 sprigs of dill, chopped
sea salt flakes and freshly
   ground black pepper

1 Heat a small, dry frying pan and toast the fenugreek, coriander and fennel seeds until fragrant, then crush them with a pinch of sea salt using a pestle and mortar.

2 Heat 2 tablespoons of the sunflower oil in a frying pan. Add the sliced onion and cook over a medium heat, stirring from time to time, for 10–15 minutes until they are amber and sweet smelling. Add the beans and warm them through.

3 Mix together the remaining tablespoon of sunflower oil, the vinegar, sugar, crushed spices, all the herbs and salt and pepper in a bowl. Stir this through the warm beans and serve. This is equally beautiful served warm or cold.

My father lived with his uncle and his Armenian wife in Azerbaijan for a year when he was 12. When I asked him what he remembers most from his time in Baku, he said it was green *lobi* (beans), a mountain of fresh coriander, dill, mint and cress salad leaves adorning the table and women baking the thin sheets of lavash bread in deep turun ovens, which are similar to Indian tandoor ovens. I have found a beautiful man selling these yellow, purple and green runner beans, which he grows on his allotment, but you can use any fresh bean you like.

Лобі | *Lobi*
Armenian beans with a tomato dressing

Serves 2

300g (10oz) mixed runner beans or French beans, sliced into 2cm (½in) lengths
2 tablespoons water
1 white onion, thinly sliced
1 beef tomato (skin discarded), roughly grated
1 garlic clove, crushed
sea salt flakes and freshly ground black pepper

1 Put the beans in a saucepan with the measurement water. Place the sliced onion on top, cover the pan with a lid and cook over a medium-low heat for 10 minutes.

2 Mix the grated tomato with the garlic and season well with salt and pepper. Dress the warm beans and onion with the garlicky tomato pulp and serve warm or cold.

This is a very simple Ukrainian starter that we often make and it has become one of my favourite canapé dishes. We also add slices of firm tomato to the filling, but texturally I prefer to use red pepper alone. Make sure the aubergines are really well charred on one side – it makes all the difference. Serve as a starter or as a side dish with Mutton in Coriander (*see* page 123).

Griddled aubergine rolls

Serves 4 as a starter or a side

2 aubergines
2 tablespoons sunflower oil
100ml (3½fl oz) soured cream
2 garlic cloves, crushed
1 red pepper, cored, deseeded and sliced into long strips
12 sprigs of dill
sea salt flakes and freshly ground black pepper

1 Slice each aubergine lengthways into slices 5mm (¼ inch) thick.

2 Brush a griddle pan with the sunflower oil and pop the aubergines on in batches. Chargrill them well on each side until lovely deep griddle marks appear and they soften enough to be rolled. You will need to keep brushing your griddle pan with oil if it goes dry.

3 Mix the soured cream and garlic together in a bowl and season it well with salt and pepper. Brush a thin layer of this over one side of each aubergine slice.

4 Place 2 strips of pepper and a dill sprig at the bottom end of each slice and roll it up, then serve.

You should try cabbage wedges the way they are roasted here – absolutely delicious. Feel free to add any old vegetable that's hanging out in your refrigerator. This is great sprinkled with some feta and served with *Kurka levengi* (*see* page 125).

Armenian roasted vegetables

Serves 4 as a side

150g (5oz) cabbage, sliced into 3 wedges (keep the core in – it's the best bit)
1 carrot, peeled and thickly sliced
1 courgette, thickly sliced
2 celery sticks, thickly sliced
1 small onion, quartered
200g (7oz) cauliflower, stalks and florets chopped
1 red pepper, cored, deseeded and roughly chopped
3 tablespoons olive oil
1 beef tomato, thickly sliced
1 tablespoon chopped dill
sea salt flakes and freshly ground black pepper

1 Preheat the oven to 200°C/400°F/Gas Mark 6. Place all the vegetables except the tomato in a large roasting tin.

2 Pour over the oil and season well with salt and pepper. Mix everything together with your hands and pop in the oven for 30 minutes until the edges of the vegetables start to char.

3 Arrange the tomato slices on top, season and place in the oven for another 15 minutes. Sprinkle over the chopped dill and serve.

This is a really light and flavoursome summer pickle. We used to eat it as salad, but it would also be lovely served as a relish – simply dice the cucumber instead of slicing it. We don't really use the long sort of cucumber in Ukraine. Ours are always stubby and prickly, and despite the general consensus that cucumbers are best eaten refrigerator cold, there is nothing better than picking one off the vine – still aromatic and warm from the blistering summer sun.

Chilli & garlic cucumber

Serves 2

300g (10oz) fresh
  gherkins or cucumber
5g (¼oz) fine sea salt
2 teaspoons sugar
4 teaspoons white wine
  vinegar or cider vinegar
1 red chilli, sliced
2 garlic cloves, crushed
2 tablespoons unrefined
  sunflower oil
1 tablespoon chopped
  parsley
1 tablespoon chopped dill

1 Slice the gherkins or cucumber lengthways into 8 long wedges.

2 Mix the salt, sugar, vinegar, chilli and garlic together, toss the gherkins or cucumber in it and leave to marinate in the refrigerator for 30 minutes.

3 Dress with the oil and sprinkle with the chopped herbs just before serving.

In terms of importance, New Year was the equivalent of Christmas in secular USSR. Families cooked elaborate meals, drank champagne and watched festive TV concerts. This salad is one of the biggest Soviet classics, up there with Olivier (Russian salad). I love the original, where everything is boiled, but since I moved to England, I have fallen in love with roasting vegetables, so my version here is a little different.

Вінегрет | *Vinegret*
Beetroot & gherkin salad

Serves 4

2 tablespoons sunflower oil
500g (1lb) beetroot, peeled and diced into 5mm (¼ inch) cubes
300g (10oz) Maris Piper potatoes, peeled and diced into 5mm (¼ inch) cubes
50g (2oz) frozen peas, blanched in boiling water for 2 minutes and drained
½ red onion, finely diced
1 large gherkin, diced
2 tablespoons unrefined sunflower oil
sea salt flakes and freshly ground black pepper

1 Preheat the oven to 180°C/350°F/Gas Mark 4.

2 Mix the regular sunflower oil with the beetroot and potatoes, pop them on a baking sheet and season well with salt and pepper. Roast for 40 minutes or until starting to caramelize slightly.

3 Let the beets and potatoes cool, then mix with the rest of the ingredients and taste for seasoning.

This is a quintessential Ukrainian village dish. Onions are traditional but recently my aunt started growing shallots and nothing crisps up better than them. This is delicious and utterly satisfying. Serve it with a roast chicken and a simple tomato salad.

Potatoes with pork & shallots

Serves 2

400g (13oz) new potatoes, peeled but kept whole
100g (3½oz) *Salo* (*see* page 136) or pancetta, sliced into lardons
100g (3½oz) shallots, sliced
sea salt flakes

1 Boil the potatoes in a saucepan of salted water for 45 minutes or until cooked but not falling apart.

2 Meanwhile, place the lardons in a dry frying pan and cook over a medium heat until they start to release some fat.

3 Add the shallots to the pan and stir from time to time for about 10–15 minutes or until crispy.

4 Drain the potatoes into a serving bowl, then pour over the lardons and shallots.

Goats are huge where I come from. They are superstars. They are everywhere. Every Sunday morning, the neighbour's goat would come and graze right underneath my window, bleeting its annoying goat song. Yet we don't really cook them. My grandmother apparently slow-cooked goat, but these days they are mainly used for milk. Raw goats' milk was my biggest nightmare, but here I am bringing the more palatable side of goatiness to Ukraine's favourite potato cakes. They are amazing served with some roast duck and Blackberry Sauce (*see* page 177).

Деруни | *Deruny*
Potato cakes with goats' cheese

Serves 2 as a side

500g (1lb) floury potatoes, peeled and roughly grated
1 small onion, roughly grated
1 small carrot, peeled and roughly grated
1 egg, lightly beaten
3 tablespoons plain flour
30g (1oz) goats' cheese, mashed with a fork
2 tablespoons sunflower oil
fine sea salt and freshly ground black pepper

1 Preheat the oven to 180°C/350°F/Gas Mark 4 and line a baking sheet with some baking parchment

2 Mix everything except the oil together in a bowl and season really well with salt and pepper.

3 Heat the oil in a large frying pan, drop separate dessertspoonfuls of the mixture into the pan and fry them for 2 minutes. Carefully flip them over and fry on the other side until golden.

4 Pop the potato cakes on the prepared baking sheet and finish cooking them through in the oven – they should take 5–10 minutes.

Traditionally, we use firm white cabbage leaves here, so if you want more of a traditional taste, please use those instead of the Savoy I've suggested. They just may need to be blanched for three minutes instead of two. My grandmother also used to make a version of this without tomatoes and using whole sauerkraut leaves (*see* page 148) and pork belly. The combination of sharp cabbage and luscious pork is incredible. I add barberries to my *holubtsi* to achieve that sour note, but you don't have to if they are hard to find.

Голубці | *Holubtsi*
Stuffed cabbage leaves

Serves 6 (makes 12 parcels)

2 tablespoons sunflower oil
1 large onion, finely diced
1 carrot, peeled and grated
1 teaspoon caster sugar
1 tablespoon tomato purée
1 fresh bay leaf
400g (13oz) can chopped tomatoes
400ml (14fl oz) water
1 Savoy cabbage, 12 leaves separated
250g (8oz) minced beef
250g (8oz) minced pork
160g (5½oz) white long-grain rice,
    parboiled for 5 minutes and drained
40g (1½oz) barberries (optional)
sea salt flakes and freshly ground
    black pepper

To serve
½ small bunch of dill, finely chopped
100ml (3½fl oz) soured cream
sourdough bread

1 Make the sauce first. Heat the sunflower oil in a heavy-based flameproof casserole dish. Fry half the onion and all the grated carrot over a medium heat for 5–10 minutes until soft. Add the sugar and the tomato purée and cook for 1 minute. Add the bay leaf, tomatoes and measurement water and season well with salt and pepper.

2 Blanch the cabbage leaves for 2 minutes in boiling water, then refresh them in cold water and drain well on kitchen paper.

3 Mix the minced meats, parboiled rice, barberries, if using, seasoning and the remaining diced onion together in a bowl. Place 50g (2oz) of the filling on to each cabbage leaf and fold up into parcels.

4 Place the parcels on top of the sauce, folded side down, tucking them next to each other snugly so that they don't unravel. Cook over a low heat for about 45 minutes or until cooked through.

5 Serve with the chopped dill, a dollop of soured cream on the side and sourdough bread.

My mum would start making this salad in April–May when the first cucumbers would come out. Prickly, gnarled, filling the air with an intense aroma, the smell of Ukrainian cucumbers freshly picked from our allotment will never leave me. The best part was dipping our bread into the remainder of the pastel pink soured cream dressing.

Spring radish & tomato salad

Serves 4

4 small cucumbers
or 1 large
2 beef tomatoes
½ bunch of radishes,
sliced
1 spring onion, sliced
½ bunch of dill, chopped

100ml (3½floz) *smetana*
or natural yogurt,
diluted with ½ tablespoon
water
sea salt flakes and freshly
ground black pepper

1 Slice the cucumbers and tomatoes over the bowl you will serve the salad in. You want to catch the tomato juices that will end up making the dressing so special.

2 Mix all the vegetables and dill together in the bowl. Season the *smetana* or yogurt really well with salt and pepper and stir through the salad. By the time you finish the salad there will be a delicious candy-floss pool of *smetana* or yogurt stained by tomato juices and radishes – mop it up with some bread.

There are roughly half a million Koreans living in Central Asia, Russia and southern Ukraine. It was hard to find Chinese cabbage in the USSR, so kimchi gradually turned into a carrot pickle. It's very different from the original kimchi, but still delicious.

Морковча| *Morkovcha*
Korean carrots

Makes a 500ml (17fl oz) jar

500g (1lb) carrots, peeled
and grated or julienned
into long strips
1 heaped teaspoon fine
sea salt
1 tablespoon caster sugar
1 tablespoon red wine
vinegar
2 large garlic cloves,
crushed

2 tablespoons sunflower
oil
½ onion, thinly sliced
1 teaspoon fennel seeds,
toasted and ground
1 teaspoon coriander
seeds, toasted and
ground
½–¼ teaspoon cayenne
pepper, or to taste

1 Mix the carrots with the salt in a ceramic or glass bowl and let them stand for an hour or so at room temperature.

2 Add the sugar, vinegar and garlic and mix well.

3 Heat the sunflower oil in a frying pan, add the onion, ground fennel and coriander seeds and cayenne and cook for about 15 minutes over a low–medium heat until the onion is very soft and slightly caramelized, then remove from the heat and let it cool.

4 Add the cooked onion to the carrots and massage everything again. The carrots will keep in a sterilized jar in the refrigerator for a month or even longer.

Tipakatz means 'lightly stewed', and this particular version of the dish comes from the Armenian area of Karabakh in Azerbaijan. In Yerevan, the capital of Armenia, this dish is sometimes baked with the eggs in the oven.

Лобі тіпакац | *Lobi tipakatz*

Armenian beans with egg & herbs

**Serves 4 as a side
or 2 as a light lunch**

500g (1lb) runner beans
1 mild white onion, sliced
2 tablespoons chopped
    dill
2 tablespoons chopped
    parsley
2 tablespoons chopped
    fresh coriander
2 eggs, lightly beaten
2 tablespoons sunflower
    or olive oil
sea salt flakes and freshly
    ground black pepper

1 Top and tail the runner beans, then slice them on the diagonal and place them in a saucepan with 1 tablespoon of water. Place the sliced onion on top and season well with salt and pepper. Cover the pan with a lid and cook over a low heat for 10 minutes.

2 Mix the herbs with the eggs and season them well with salt and pepper, then add them to the pan and give it all a good stir. Raise the heat slightly and leave to cook for 5 minutes or until the eggs are set. Serve this warm or cold.

We don't traditionally use sunflower seeds in this way in Ukraine. We just fry them in their shells and then pop them into our mouths, expertly cracking the shells with our teeth and popping the seeds out with our tongues. I must have eaten kilos and kilos of sunflower seeds throughout my childhood, so I miss them and the cosy evenings in the kitchen reading by candlelight (there used to be regular power cuts) and munching the seeds. Don't throw away the cabbage core – slice it and roast it with the Armenian Roasted Vegetables on page 74.

Cabbage slaw with toasted sunflower seeds

Serves 4

2 tablespoons unrefined
  sunflower oil
½ tablespoon white wine
  vinegar
½ teaspoon caster sugar
½ small red onion, thinly
  sliced
1 small white cabbage,
  thinly sliced
2 carrots, peeled and
  grated or julienned
sea salt flakes

To serve
20g (¾oz) sunflower
  seeds, toasted
1 tablespoon chopped dill

1 Mix the sunflower oil, vinegar and sugar together in a salad bowl, and season to taste with salt. Add the onion and let it sit in the dressing for 5 minutes.

2 Add the other vegetables and mix together, then garnish with the toasted sunflower seeds and chopped dill.

Courgettes and beautiful flat summer squashes grow in abundance in Ukraine. I remember finding this on the summer kitchen stove – Mum having made it for our lunch in the morning before going to work. It's even better the next day and I like eating it cold. *Sous* literally means 'sauce' and I really enjoy dipping bread into it, collecting pieces of melting, slow-cooked courgette.

Соус | *Sous*

Courgette & potato stew

Serves 4

4–6 tablespoons sunflower oil
500g (1lb) courgettes, sliced
50g (2oz) plain flour
250g (8oz) potatoes, peeled and thinly sliced
1 onion, thinly sliced
1 tablespoon tomato purée
2 garlic cloves, crushed
500g (1lb) beef tomatoes (skin discarded), grated
100ml (3½fl oz) water
100ml (3½fl oz) soured cream
½ bunch of dill, chopped
sea salt flakes and freshly ground black pepper
toasted bread, to serve

1 Heat some of the sunflower oil in a heavy-based frying pan. Toss the courgette slices in the flour, shake the excess off and fry them over a medium heat on both sides until nicely caramelized. Do this in batches, adding some extra oil each time if the pan is looking a bit dry. When done, remove the courgettes on to kitchen paper to absorb the excess oil.

2 Now fry the potatoes in the pan, without flouring them, for about 5 minutes on each side until they begin to colour nicely.

3 Add the onion and tomato purée to the same pan and cook over a medium-low heat, stirring often, for about 10 minutes until the onion starts to soften and caramelize ever so slightly. Then lower the heat, add the garlic and cook for another minute.

4 Place the courgettes back into the pan and add the tomato pulp, measurement water and soured cream and stir gently to combine. Season very well with salt and pepper and bring to the boil.

5 Lower the heat and simmer for 30 minutes or until the potatoes are cooked and the liquid is slightly reduced. Sprinkle with the dill and serve with toasted bread to mop up the juices.

I cannot rave enough about the quantity and quality of tomatoes in the south of Ukraine. The summers are so hot that the fruit we grow is everything that a perfect tomato should be – sweet, meaty but also juicy and with that knockout woody smell of the vines. I nearly included five different recipes for fermenting tomatoes but then I restrained myself and now you only have two (see also page 157–8). This cooked tomato recipe is amazing though. I would seek out a little bit of *twaróg* for this instead of feta and season it to your taste – it will create a lovely golden crust. Look out for an Eastern European grocery shop, or online food supplier, which will normally sell *twaróg*, the equivalent of our Ukrainian homemade curd cheese, *Syr* (*see* page 109). Pick whatever herbs you like to mix into it. I imagine basil would be a natural match, but me – I just can't live without dill...

Tomatoes stuffed with cheese & herbs

Serves 4

4 beef tomatoes
200g (7oz) Polish *twaróg*
  or *Syr* (*see* page 109),
  or use feta cheese
2 tablespoons chopped
  dill
1 tablespoon chopped
  parsley
1 teaspoon sunflower oil
sea salt flakes and freshly
  ground black pepper

1 Preheat the oven to 180°C/350°F/Gas Mark 4.

2 Cut the tops off the tomatoes and hollow them out, taking out the core but making sure you keep the tomatoes intact.

3 Mix the cheese, herbs and seasoning together, then stuff the tomatoes with the mixture.

4 Use the sunflower oil to lightly oil the bottom of a baking sheet, pop the tomatoes on and bake for 30–35 minutes or until the tomatoes are soft and the cheese turns golden.

Вареники та локшина
Dumplings & Noodles

This dish must have a German origin, as there is something similar called *strudli*, except sauerkraut is used in place of the potatoes. My great-grandmother cooked it and we suspect she picked it up in Bessarabia (where Moldova met Ukraine). It's hearty, yes, but it's also the best dumpling recipe I know.

Нудлі / *Nudli*
Pork ribs & dumplings

Serves 8–10 as a feast

2 tablespoons sunflower oil
1kg (2lb) pork ribs, cut into individual ribs
500g (1lb) potatoes, peeled and
 quartered lengthways
1 large onion, sliced
50ml (2fl oz) apple juice or wine
750ml–1 litre (1¼–1¾ pints) water
1 bay leaf
sea salt flakes and freshly ground
 black pepper
Sour Gherkins or Sour Aubergines
 (*see* page 152), to serve

Dumplings
2 x recipe quantities of *Kefir* Dough
 (*see* page 48)
plain flour, for dusting
4 tablespoons sunflower oil

1 Heat the sunflower oil in a large, heavy-based flameproof casserole dish. Season the ribs with salt and pepper and brown them really well over a high heat in batches, making sure they colour nicely. Lift them out and set aside. Don't wipe the pan out.

2 Add the potatoes to the pan and brown well on each side. Add the onion, lower the heat and sweat for 10 minutes or until soft. Add the apple juice or wine and deglaze the pan.

3 Place the meat and its juices back in the pan and pour over enough of the measurement water to cover. Add the bay leaf, season with salt and pepper and cook over a low heat for 2 hours or until the meat starts falling off the bones.

4 Meanwhile, make the *Kefir* dough and divide it into 4 pieces. Flour the work surface really generously and roll out one piece of the dough into a rectangle 2mm (slightly less than ⅛ inch) thick. Pour 1 tablespoon of the sunflower oil over it and rub it all over with your hand. Roll the dough up into a thick sausage shape. Twist it gently at both ends as you would if you were ringing out clothes (how retro!). Repeat with the remaining dough and oil.

5 Slice each dough sausage across into 5cm (2 inch) pieces. You should end up with about 35 dumplings.

6 Now check how much liquid there is in the stew. It should be still wet, but not too much. You want your dumpling bottoms to absorb some of the juices but their tops should steam.

7 Whack up the heat in your stew. My gran used to call this 'breathing strength' into it. It should be boiling like crazy.

8 Now swiftly but gently pop the dumplings into the stew. Once they are all in, pop the lid over. No steam should escape, so place a folded wet tea towel around the rim of the lid if you see steam escaping. Cook over a high heat for 15 minutes, then lower the heat and cook for another 30 minutes. Serve with Sour Gherkins or Sour Aubergines.

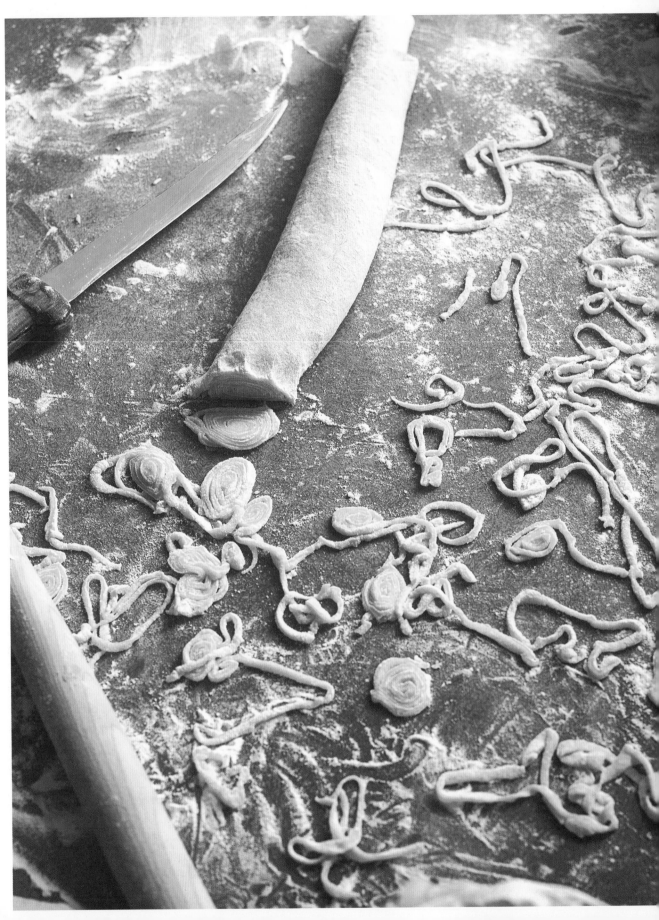

This is our equivalent of Italian pasta. I sometimes buy Italian eggs when I make noodles, as their gorgeous, deep-coloured yolks turn the pasta dough into an incredibly rich yellow. We normally roll this out by hand, but if you have a pasta machine, I don't see why you shouldn't use it.

Noodle dough

Makes 500g (1lb)

5 eggs – the best quality you can get

300–400g (10–13oz) '00' pasta flour, plus extra for dusting

1 Lightly beat the eggs in a bowl, then slowly sift in and mix in the flour – just enough to create a firm dough.

2 Knead the dough until it becomes firm and elastic without sticking – then cover with clingfilm and let it rest at room temperature for about 30 minutes.

3 Flour your work surface generously. Divide the dough into 4 pieces and roll each piece out as thinly as you can.

This dish is a love child of the USSR's far-flung bribery and *autarkic* shortcomings. My Aunt Zhenia's husband was a surgeon. Soviet healthcare was free, but a tasty or an intoxicating bribe to speed things up has always been standard practice. My Uncle was often presented with a freshly plucked goose, so fresh that its skin still smelled of singed feathers. As for the *autarky*, Soviet shops were empty at the best of times and the only pasta you could get was a grey-tinged macaroni that disintegrated on touching boiling water. So my aunt made her own noodles. This dish is something our whole extended family adopted: silky noodles, pulled goose and its juices. So simple yet so satisfying. This recipe also works well with duck – a French mallard may work better here than the fat old Gressingham.

Локшина з гускою | *Lapsha z guskoyu*
Soviet goose noodles

Serves 4

I small goose or I large
   duck, jointed
IOOml (3½fl oz) water
I recipe quantity of
   Noodle Dough (*see*
   page IO2)
sea salt flakes and freshly
   ground black pepper
green salad or Fermented
   Tomatoes (*see* page I57),
   to serve

I Place the goose pieces in a large, heavy-based flameproof casserole dish. Don't use any oil, and don't preheat the casserole – this will ensure that the fat is rendered slowly. Fry the pieces gently on all sides until brown and a lot of the fat has been rendered. You may need to do this in batches

2 If there is a lot of fat, skim some of it off, then add the water, season the meat well with salt and pepper and cook over the lowest heat possible, covered tightly, for 2 hours or until tender and you can easily pull the meat off the bones.

3 Meanwhile, make the noodle dough.

4 Roll up each sheet of dough into a tube and cut across into 5mm (¼ inch) noodles. Leave the noodles to dry for 30–60 minutes. Once the goose is ready, cook the noodles in a large saucepan of salted boiling water for 2 minutes.

5 Either serve the meat pieces on top of the noodles, or pull the meat from the bones and mix it with the juices from the goose, then add the noodles to the meat and give them a good stir to coat them well. Serve with a simple green salad with a lemony dressing or some Fermented Tomatoes.

This is my death row wish, my last supper, my ultimate source of comfort. I had trouble deciding how many people the recipes below would serve – I can eat 40 dumplings at one sitting, and that is no joke. It may be nostalgia or that they are so incredibly tasty, or perhaps I am just a glutton. If you have any *varenyky* left over, they are amazing the next day, fried in butter until crispy.

Вареники | *Varenyky*
Stuffed Ukrainian pasta

**All serve 4 or
1 hungry Ukrainian
(makes 40–50 dumplings)**

Water dough
1 large egg, lightly beaten
150ml (¼ pint) water
300–350g (10–11½oz)
  '00' or plain flour,
  plus extra for dusting
fine sea salt

Curd cheese filling
Varenyky z syrom
150g (5oz) *Syr* (*see* page
  109) or Polish *twaróg*
1 egg, lightly beaten
50g (2oz) butter, melted
50ml (2fl oz) soured
  cream or creamy Greek
  yogurt, to serve

Cabbage filling
Varenyky z kapustoyu
1 tablespoon sunflower oil
300g (10oz) *Kvashena
  kapusta* (*see* page 148)
50g (2oz) butter, melted
50ml (2fl oz) soured
  cream or creamy Greek
  yogurt, to serve

1 First make the dough. Mix the egg and water together in a bowl, then gradually add the flour and mix it in well; if you feel that there isn't enough flour, add slightly more than the recipe states.

2 Knead the dough on a well-floured work surface until it stops sticking to your hands. What you are looking for is a firm (or as we call it in Ukraine, tight), elastic dough.

3 Wrap the dough in clingfilm and rest in the refrigerator for 30 minutes to help the gluten relax.

4 Next make your chosen filling.

For the curd cheese filling, mix the cheese and egg together in a bowl and season heavily with salt – it should be slightly oversalted.

For the cabbage filling, heat the sunflower oil in a large frying pan and gently fry the cabbage for 5 minutes. Place it in a bowl and let it cool completely.

For the potato filling, place the potatoes in a saucepan and cover with cold water, season well with salt and bring them to the boil. Cook for 15 minutes or until they can be easily pierced with a knife. Drain the potatoes and mash them really well.

Meanwhile, heat the sunflower oil in a frying pan and fry the shallots over a medium-low heat for about 15–20 minutes until starting to colour nicely. Mix the shallots with the potatoes and set aside.

Place the lardons in a dry frying pan and fry them over a medium heat until crispy. Tip them into a bowl and set aside.

Potato filling with crispy pork *Varenyky z kartopleyu*

150g (5oz) potatoes, peeled and chopped

2 tablespoons sunflower oil

100g (3½oz) shallots, sliced

100g (2oz) *Salo* (*see* page 136) or pancetta, sliced into lardons

sea salt flakes

5 Divide the dough into 2 pieces. Flour your work surface generously and roll out the dough into a 30cm (12 inch) diameter circle or until the dough is a bit less than 2mm (about ¹⁄₁₆ inch) thick. Cut the dough into 3cm (1¼ inch) squares – you should end up with about 20–25. Don't throw away the offcuts. These can be cooked along with the stuffed pasta.

6 Repeat with the second piece of dough.

7 Have a well-floured tray ready. Pop 1 teaspoon of the filling into the centre of each square, fold in half diagonally to create a triangular-shaped dumpling and press the edges together to seal. Place the *varenyky* on the floured tray, making sure that they don't touch each other.

8 For the curd cheese- and cabbage-filled *varenyky*, have a large bowl with the melted butter ready.

9 Bring a large saucepan of salted water to the boil and carefully pop the *varenyky* in. Boil them for a couple of minutes or until they float to the surface.

10 Drain the *varenyky* well. For the curd cheese and cabbage *varenyky*, tip them into the melted butter and swirl them around, then serve with the soured cream or Greek yogurt. For the potato with crispy pork *varenyky*, sprinkle over the lardons and pour over any fat and serve.

Almost every week my mum used to suspend a muslin cloth with milk curds over the sink and the next morning we had *syr* (which literally means 'cheese' in Ukrainian). Her mother did the same, as did her grandmother and so on. Eaten with some *smetana* soured cream and fresh raspberries for breakfast, or used in numerous sweet and savoury dishes, it's a dairy product that I cannot live without. The process may seem a little complicated (it isn't!), and raw milk is not that easy to come by, but more and more farmers' markets sell it. The satisfaction gained from making your own cheese will certainly be worth the effort.

Сир | *Syr*
Curd cheese

Makes about 300g (10oz) *Syr* and 1.3 litres (2¼ pints) whey

1.7 litres (2¾ pints) raw
   (unpasteurized) milk

You will also need a piece of muslin

1 Leave the raw milk in a 2-litre (3½-pint) jar to go sour in a warm place in your kitchen. Check it after 24 hours. The milk should become thick like Greek yogurt but it should still be homogenous – the whey shouldn't separate from the cream. It may take up to 2 days.

2 When the milk has soured and thickened, place half an empty egg box at the bottom of a large, deep saucepan and pop the jar of soured milk, uncovered, on top of it. Then fill the pan with water to go as far up the outer sides of the jar as possible.

3 Bring to the boil, then lower the heat and simmer for an hour or until the whey separates from the cream and you can see thick cracks forming along the sides.

4 Take the jar out carefully and leave to cool down a little.

5 While still warm, drain the curds through a muslin cloth set in a sieve over a large bowl, then leave overnight in the refrigerator. You can tie the corners of the muslin cloth together into a bag and weight it down a bit – this will help get rid of the moisture more quickly. Don't throw away the whey – you can use it to make flatbreads (*see* page 49), so simply pour it into a clean jar and keep it in the refrigerator. Use both within 1 week.

NOTE: To make a drier, salted version of this cheese (to use as you would feta), add 5g (¼oz) fine sea salt to the drained curds – it should taste quite salty, almost slightly oversalted, so add more salt if necessary. Place the curds in a clean muslin cloth, tie it at the top and weight it down on a tray. Leave in the refrigerator for a day or two before using.

These dumplings may originally be a Chinese dish that has been adopted by many a Turkic people in Central Asia. Using pork in this recipe may be sacrilege (originally fat-rumped lamb would have been used), but this is the way we make them and I will stick to the Ukrainian version this time since I love pork belly. They should be eaten with your hands, and you should try and catch the juices that accumulate inside. This requires a bit of practice, as they are eaten hot.

Манти | *Manty*

Tartar steamed dumplings

Serves 4 hungry people (makes 20)

250g (8oz) boneless pork belly or shoulder
150g (5oz) onion, finely diced
1 recipe quantity of Water Dough (*see* page 106)
about 50g (2oz) butter
sunflower or other flavourless oil, for oiling
fine sea salt and freshly ground black pepper
melted butter, to serve

1 Slice the pork into thin strips and then cut it across as finely as you can. You are basically making hand-chopped mince here. Add the onion to the meat in a bowl, season really well with salt and mix thoroughly with your hands.

2 Divide the Water Dough into 2 pieces and roll each piece into a sausage shape. Cut each sausage into 10 x 25g (1oz) pieces.

3 Roll each piece into a rough 12cm (5-inch) square. Place 1 tablespoon of the meat mixture in the centre of each square and a tiny piece of the butter on top of the filling. Pull up 2 edges of the square and press them firmly together above the meat. Do the same with the 2 other edges, creating an X shape with the edges. Now join the 'ears' by joining the corners, turning the X shape into a ∞ shape.

4 Lightly oil your steamer and pop the *manty* in. Steam them for 45–50 minutes or until the filling inside is cooked. Serve with some melted butter and plenty of pepper.

This is a strange one in the sense that it's hard to classify this dish. My mum would make this for us for breakfast, sprinkled with sugar. I drench mine in maple syrup, but runny honey would also be good. You can also eat this unsweetened for lunch.

Галушки | *Halushky*

Ukrainian gnocchi

Serves 2

150g (5oz) *Syr* (*see* page 109) or Polish *twaróg*
1 egg, lightly beaten
50g (2oz) plain flour, plus extra for dusting
10g (⅓oz) butter, melted
fine sea salt

To serve

4 teaspoons soured cream or Greek yogurt
1 tablespoon maple syrup (optional)

1 Mix the cheese and egg together in a bowl and season well with salt (taste it – it should be slightly oversalted).

2 Add the flour and mix well with a fork.

3 Meanwhile, flour your work surface really well and knead the dough for 1 minute. Shape the dough into a sausage with the palms of your hands, starting from the middle and stretching the dough outwards, like you would when making gnocchi. Finally, cut the sausage into 25 pillowy dumplings.

4 Bring a large saucepan of salted water to the boil. Have a large bowl with the melted butter ready. Pop the dumplings into the pan of boiling water and cook for about 2 minutes until they float to the surface. Drain well, add them to the melted butter and serve with the soured cream or Greek yogurt, and maple syrup, if you like.

Beshbarmak means 'with five fingers', as Turkic nomads used to use the pasta sheets instead of cutlery to pick up the meat and onions. My grandmother picked this recipe up when she lived in Tashkent. The original is usually made with fat-rump lambs but when she moved to Ukraine she adapted it by using chickens. It is a celebratory but also simple dish in terms of the amount of ingredients used, so it is worth finding the best-quality chicken and eggs.

Бешбармак | *Beshbarmak*
Central Asian chicken & pasta

Serves 6

1 small but plump
   organic chicken, about
   1.25kg (2½lb)
1 bay leaf
10 black peppercorns
5 allspice berries
500g (1lb) onions or
   shallots, thinly sliced
1 recipe quantity of
   Noodle Dough
   (*see* page 102)
plain flour, for dusting
fine sea salt and freshly
   ground black pepper

1 Place the chicken in a large saucepan and cover with cold water. Add the bay leaf, peppercorns, allspice and a pinch of salt and bring to the boil. Lower the heat and simmer the chicken for 1 hour or until it starts falling off the bone. While the chicken is simmering, keep skimming the fat off the top and pour it into a medium saucepan. You will cook your onions in that.

2 When the chicken is cooked through, drain it into a large bowl, reserving the stock, and let the meat cool, then take the meat off the bone.

3 Place the onions in the saucepan of chicken fat with some salt and pepper and cook over a low heat for 1 hour until they become meltingly soft.

4 Meanwhile, make the noodle dough, then roll out into 4 sheets following the instructions on page 102.

5 Have a well-floured tray ready. Cut each pasta sheet into strips about 5cm (2 inches) wide and then cut each strip into diamonds about 5cm (2 inches) across.

6 Mix the chicken with the onions and gently reheat.

7 Bring the reserved chicken stock to the boil, pop in your pasta and cook for 2 minutes until tender. Drain the pasta and mix it with the onions and meat, then serve.

This is an incredibly comforting dish. If you love polenta, you will fall in love with this, too. In western Ukraine, the Hutsul people make something very similar and call it *banosh*. Any leftovers can be sautéed in butter until crispy.

Мамалига | *Mamalyga*
Moldovan polenta

Serves 2 as a main

750ml (1¼ pints) water
50g (2oz) butter
175g (6oz) coarse yellow cornmeal
100g (3½oz) *Salo* (*see page 136*) or pancetta, sliced into lardons
100g (3½oz) salty sheep's cheese, crumbled
fine sea salt and freshly ground black pepper

1 Fill a large saucepan with the measurement water, add the butter, season with salt and pepper and bring to the boil.

2 Add the cornmeal in a continuous, gentle stream, stirring all the time over a low heat. Keep stirring for about 10 minutes, then put on the lowest heat possible and cover with a lid. Cook for 20 minutes, stirring occasionally so it doesn't stick to the pan. It will also start forming baby volcanoes, so watch out that it doesn't spit in your face.

3 Let the *mamalyga* rest in the pan for 10 minutes, then turn it out on to a plate.

4 Meanwhile, add the lardons to a cold dry frying pan and fry until crispy.

5 My grandmothers used a thread to cut the *mamalyga*. You can use a knife if you prefer. Then pinch a little bit with your fingers and dip it into the cheese or lardons, or both!

М'ясо та риба
Meat & Fish

My Aunt Nina's introduction to this dish was: 'This plov is never cooked for funerals, only weddings!', and it's definitely a happy occasion dish. Every Azerbaijani wedding that she went to, if she knew this pilau was coming, she would wait for it patiently and wouldn't eat anything else. It takes some time to make, but the result is totally worth it. The meat is cooked separately from the rice.

Азербайджанський плов | *Azerbaydzhans'kyy plov*

Azerbaijani rice & fruity lamb

Serves 4

750g (1½lb) boneless mutton or lamb neck or shoulder, diced
350g (11½oz) onions, sliced
75g (3oz) pitted prunes, soaked in water
75g (3oz) dried apricots
75g (3oz) sultanas
sea salt flakes and freshly ground black pepper

Rice

450g (14½oz) white long-grain rice
100g (3½oz) plain flour
½ teaspoon fine sea salt
2 eggs, lightly beaten
150g (5oz) clarified butter or ghee
large pinch of saffron threads
1 teaspoon ground cumin (optional)

1 Wash the meat but don't dry it. Place it in a large, dry saucepan, season with plenty of salt and pepper, cover with a lid and cook over a very low heat for about 1½ hours. The meat will cook in its own juices and should be falling apart by the end of the cooking time.

2 When the meat is close to its melt-in-the-mouth consistency, add the onions and cook over a low heat , stirring occasionally, for about 20–30 minutes until caramelized.

3 If dry, add some water with the dried fruit and cook, covered, for another 30 minutes.

4 Meanwhile, prepare the rice. Bring a large saucepan of water to the boil. Add the rice and season well with salt. Give the rice a good stir and parboil it for 5 minutes. It should still be al dente. Drain the rice and spread it over a baking sheet to cool a little and to stop it from cooking further.

5 Now make the *gazmakh*, which is the crispy rice shell that will adorn the pilau when you turn it out. Mix the flour, fine sea salt and the eggs together in a bowl, then add 100g (3½oz) of the parboiled rice and mix everything really well. It should look like a thick batter.

6 To assemble the *plov*, wash the rice pan out and add 25g (1oz) of the clarified butter or ghee. Heat it well and then add the *gazmakh* batter making sure it covers the whole base of your pan (a larger base will make for a thinner crust). I use an oiled hand to spread it out, but I recommend you use a spatula. Cook it for 1 minute until it catches a bit.

7 Put the saffron and cumin, if using, into the rest of the clarified butter or ghee and let it stand. Spoon the parboiled rice over the *gazmakh*.

8 Make holes in the *plov* using the handle of a wooden spoon and pour over the spiced butter. Cover the pan with a tight-fitting lid and wrap it with a damp tea towel around the edges as well. No steam should escape! Cook the rice for about 45 minutes over the lowest heat possible, checking after 30 minutes.

9 To serve, place the rice on a large round platter. Gently lift out the crispy bottom, break it into shards and serve on top of the rice. Place the lamb, fruit and its juice around the rice.

This is a dish that my Ossetian friend gave to me a while back. It's slightly modernized, as they would never use soy sauce or ginger in Ossetian food, but both definitely enhance it. Adding fresh garlic at the end is a typical ploy in the Caucasus region. I know it seems crazy to cook fresh herbs for such a long time, but it works, and when you add the fresh herb leaves at the end, it all sings.

Mutton in coriander

Serves 4

80g (3oz) coriander, roots, stalks and leaves
80g (3oz) parsley, stalks and leaves
25g (1oz) dill, stalks and leaves
25g (1oz) fresh root ginger, peeled
1 fresh bay leaf
2 tablespoons pomegranate molasses
2 tablespoons soy sauce
1 tablespoon clear honey
1 teaspoon piri piri sauce
750g (1½lb) mutton or lamb ribs, cut into individual ribs
1 large onion, thinly sliced
2 carrots, peeled and grated
2 beef tomatoes (skin discarded), grated
1 green pepper, cored, deseeded and chopped
2 garlic cloves, crushed
sea salt flakes and freshly ground black pepper

1 Wash the herbs, especially the coriander stalks and roots. Blitz the stalks (reserve the leaves) with the ginger, bay leaf, pomegranate molasses, soy sauce, honey and piri piri in a food processor.

2 Rub the herb mixture over the ribs and onion in a bowl, cover with clingfilm and place in the refrigerator to marinate for a couple of hours or preferably overnight.

3 The next day, place the ribs and their marinade in a large saucepan, add the carrots and tomato pulp, season with salt and pepper, then cook over a low heat for a couple of hours or until the meat is very tender.

4 When it is almost ready, add the green pepper and garlic and the herb leaves, chopped. Cook for 5 minutes and then serve.

Oh how they love walnuts in the Caucasus and how they love their Alycha plums, which are turned into a lovely sour sauce. Prunes will never be the perfect match; they are too sweet, hence my addition of lemon. But this works as a delicious alternative to your regular roast chicken. *Levengi* means 'inside the stomach', and it is used to stuff both poultry and fish. Add some spices to the stuffing and it will be almost festive. A sprinkling of sumac gives an extra sour note, and walnuts add welcome texture.

Курка левенгі | *Kurka levengi*

Azerbaijani chicken with prunes & walnuts

Serves 6

2 tablespoons olive oil
1 medium chicken
1 tablespoon ground sumac
100g (3½oz) pitted prunes, finely chopped
grated rind and juice of 1 lemon
200g (7oz) walnuts, toasted and roughly chopped
1 red onion, grated
sea salt flakes and freshly ground black pepper
Armenian Roasted Vegetables (see page 74), to serve

1 Preheat the oven to 180°C/350°F/Gas Mark 4. Rub the olive oil all over the chicken. Place in a roasting tin and sprinkle it with the sumac.

2 Mix the prunes with lemon rind and juice, walnuts and onion, then stuff the mixture inside the chicken.

3 Roast for 1 hour or until the juices run clear when you slice through the thickest part of the leg. Serve with Armenian Roasted Vegetables.

I used to hate onions when I was little. And then I had some *kasha* (boiled buckwheat), chicken livers and onions, sweet and caramelized, and that was it – I was in love.

Chicken liver, buckwheat & crispy shallots

Serves 2 as a starter

100g (3½oz) shallots, thinly sliced
50g (2oz) plain flour
6 tablespoons sunflower oil
200g (7oz) chicken livers

Buckwheat
2 tablespoons olive oil
2 shallots, finely diced
2 garlic cloves, finely chopped
50g (2oz) celery, finely diced
1 carrot, peeled and finely diced
2 sprigs of thyme, finely chopped
100g (3½oz) buckwheat, toasted
200ml (7fl oz) vegetable or chicken stock
sea salt flakes and freshly ground black pepper
Rhubarb & Radish Pickle (*see* below), to serve

1 Dust the shallot slices in the flour. Heat 4 tablespoons of the sunflower oil in a frying pan and shallow-fry the shallots over a medium-low heat, stirring often, for 2 minutes or until they are crispy and light golden. Remove with a slotted spoon and drain on kitchen paper.

2 Meanwhile, for the buckwheat, heat the olive oil in the pan, add the diced shallots, garlic, celery, carrot and thyme and sweat them over a medium-low heat for about 10 minutes or until soft and aromatic.

3 Add the buckwheat and stock, season with salt and pepper and cook over a low heat for 20 minutes or until the buckwheat absorbs all the stock.

4 Heat the remaining sunflower oil in a frying pan, add the chicken livers and sauté for 5–8 minutes or until they are well caramelized and cooked through. Serve with the crispy shallots, buckwheat and Rhubarb & Radish Pickle.

This is one of my recipes inspired by Mum's notorious rhubarb glut. It is also amazing with grilled mackerel in a brioche bun.

Rhubarb & radish pickle

Serves 2

juice of 1 large lemon
2 teaspoons caster sugar
1 fennel bulb
150g (5oz) rhubarb
150g (5oz) radishes
sea salt flakes and freshly ground black pepper

1 Mix the lemon juice with the sugar and some salt and pepper in a medium ceramic or glass bowl.

2 Trim the fennel and remove the tough outer stalks. Reserve the fennel fronds.

3 Slice the rhubarb, radishes and fennel as thinly as you possibly can. Immediately toss them in the seasoned lemon juice to avoid oxidization and to pickle them slightly. Let them stand for 10 minutes, then add the fennel fronds and serve.

This is the most popular Georgian dish outside Georgia. The young spatchcocked chickens were traditionally cooked on special tapa skillets, weighted down with a brick. I have recently learned that in Hungary they call it 'iron chicken'. I can just picture those hefty vintage irons adorning frying pans all over Budapest, sweet garlicky smells penetrating multi-storey blocks of flats. This was the first dish my mother taught me. I was not even remotely interested in cooking then, so I burned it badly. The trick is to keep the hob on the lowest setting. As for the weight, my mother often used my dad's old-school circus dumbbell. It was probably not the safest option and I now use my huge granite mortar, but a couple of food cans should also do the job.

Курка табака | *Kurka tabaka*

Garlicky Georgian poussins

Serves 2

2 poussins
4 garlic cloves, finely
  grated
½ teaspoon cayenne
  pepper
40g (1½oz) butter
1 tablespoon sunflower
  oil
½ tablespoon chopped
  tarragon
½ tablespoon chopped
  basil
½ tablespoon chopped
  parsley
½ tablespoon chopped
  dill
sea salt flakes

To serve
good bread
Tkhemali (see page 131)

1 Spatchcock each poussin by cutting it along the backbone with a knife or scissors. Flatten them with the palm of your hand, then rub with the grated garlic and season generously all over with salt and the cayenne pepper.

2 Heat the butter and oil in a large, heavy-based skillet or frying pan. Cook the poussins, cut side down, over a medium heat for 3 minutes, then flip them over and cook them skin side down for 5 minutes.

3 Lower the heat and place a cartouche (a circle of baking parchment or greaseproof paper) over the birds, followed by a smaller frying pan on top. Weight it all down with something heavy.

4 Cook for 20–25 minutes over the lowest possible heat. To test that the poussins are cooked, pull away at the legs – they should come away easily and the juices should run clear.

5 When the birds are done, lift them out and rest on a chopping board for 5 minutes. Add the herbs to the buttery juices and cook for another minute or two.

6 Serve the poussins drizzled with the herby juices, or mop the juices up with some good bread, along with the Tkhemali.

This recipe was inspired by *tkhemali*, a sauce made from green Alycha plums, which is spicy and very tart in its original form. I add black treacle to mine because I am crazy about sweet and sour flavours. So even though this is not a true *tkhemali* sauce (please forgive me, Georgian *mamushkas*), the flavour combination of plums or greengages, smoky paprika and a hint of molasses is a winner. You can also substitute treacle with some soft dark brown sugar. Add as much sweetness as you find pleasing, or don't add any at all if your plums are very sweet.

Тхемалі | *Tkhemali*

Georgian plum chutney

Serves 4

350g (11½oz) plums or
greengages, stoned and
roughly chopped
1 garlic clove, grated or
crushed
½ teaspoon smoked
paprika
½ tablespoon black
treacle
2 sprigs of dill, chopped
sea salt flakes

1 Place the plums or greengages in a saucepan, add a splash of water, cover with a lid and boil over a medium-low heat for about 10 minutes until the fruits start to soften.

2 Mash them with a fork, then add the garlic, paprika and treacle, and season with salt.

3 Cook with the lid off for another 10 minutes.

4 Add the dill and serve at room temperature with the *Kurka tabaka* (*see* page 130). You can keep the sauce for a few days in a sterilized jar in the refrigerator. If sealed, it will keep for ages.

This is my dad's creation. He actually used apricot jam instead of honey last summer and nobody clocked where the caramelized amazingness was coming from. I am going for a less wacky honey option here. This recipe is good for using up soft herb stalks that you don't need – they are full of flavour. Throw washed coriander roots in there, too, if you get your herbs from a local grocer rather than a supermarket.

Kefir & herb barbecued chicken

Serves 6–8

1 tablespoon sunflower oil
60g (2¼ oz) coriander
    stalks and leaves,
    roughly chopped
60g (2¼oz) parsley stalks
    and leaves, roughly
    chopped
250g (8oz) *kefir* or natural
    yogurt
75g (3oz) clear honey
2 teaspoons piri piri sauce
1kg (2lb) boneless chicken
    thighs
sea salt flakes and freshly
    ground black pepper

1 To make the marinade, place all of the ingredients, except the meat, into a food processor and blitz.

2 Place the mixture into a large container and check the seasoning before you drop the chicken in. When you are happy with the sweet, salty, spice balance, add the chicken. Rub the marinade all over the chicken, cover and leave to marinate in the refrigerator for a couple of hours or preferably overnight.

3 Preheat a barbecue. Take the chicken out of the marinade and throw the pieces on the hottest part of the barbecue. Cook for 10 minutes on each side or until the juices run clear, then devour.

This ancient Slavic dish was traditionally prepared using bear meat in Russia. In the (fortunate) absence of bears, we normally use pork or beef in Ukraine. This is a dish that my parents used to make, usually for New Year's Eve celebrations; it was a little too opulent for their parents' generation. It's normally served cold as an hors d'oeuvre. Wild thyme grows happily along the banks of the Dnieper River near my parents' house, but regular or lemon thyme will do just fine.

Буженина | *Buzhenyna*

Aromatic roast pork loin

Serves 10–12 as a starter

1.5kg (3lb) solid piece of
  pork loin or neck (no
  rolled stuff!)
150g (5oz) carrots, peeled
  and cut into long strips
  5mm (¼ inch) thick
6 garlic cloves, sliced in
  half if large
½ teaspoon rock salt
leaves from 2 sprigs of
  rosemary, roughly
  chopped
3 sprigs of wild or lemon
  thyme, roughly chopped
2 tablespoons sunflower
  oil

Brine

50ml (2fl oz) water
1 teaspoon fine sea salt
1 tablespoon mixed
  peppercorns (black,
  pink, green)
1 teaspoon allspice berries

1 For the brine, place the water, salt and spices in a small saucepan. Bring to the boil but be careful not to over-reduce, then leave to cool and infuse.

2 Using a thick metal skewer or a thin knife, make long incisions in the pork neck and insert a strip of carrot into each incision. It's easier to leave the skewer in as you push the carrot in. If the pork loin piece is long, make some incisions from one end and then from the other. Repeat the 'pierce-and-stick' action with the garlic.

3 Strain the brine liquid and, using a marinade injector syringe (my mum used an old Soviet syringe with a thick needle; just thought I'd mention that), inject the aromatic brine into the pork.

4 Next, grind the rock salt with the rosemary and thyme into a paste using a pestle and mortar and mix in the sunflower oil. Rub this all over the meat in a bowl, cover with clingfilm and leave to marinate in the refrigerator overnight.

5 The next day, preheat the oven to 160°C/325°F/Gas Mark 3. Wrap the meat tightly in foil, place in a roasting tin and roast for 1½–2 hours for pork loin, longer if using pork neck, until cooked through. Let the meat cool completely, then slice and serve as part of a festive spread.

This is normally referred to as '*Ukrayinskyy narkotyk*'. I am not even joking. Ex-pats have been known to smuggle kilos of this in their suitcases when emigrating or visiting friends in America (I am not revealing any names!). It is happily eaten straight from the freezer, thinly sliced and gently balancing over some warm rye bread. *Salo*, vodka, raw garlic, tomatoes and some gherkins were offered to my friend Tom by my father, at 4:30am in a frost-bitten field, just before they went wild goose hunting. Tom said he'd never had a better breakfast. The following curing technique was kindly given to me by a beautiful butcher named Yury, from Kakhovka market. He salted some for me there and then, and I shall not be telling whether I've smuggled some out or not.

Сало | *Salo*

Ukrainian 'narcotics'

Makes 500g (1lb)

1kg (2lb) boneless
  skin-on pork belly (with
  more fat than meat)
500g (1lb) fine sea salt
5 garlic cloves, grated
  (optional)

1 Make slashes in the meat in 2 places so the meat is still attached to the skin, then cover it in salt and garlic, if using. Wrap the pork belly in clingfilm and leave to cure in the refrigerator for 3 days.

2 Wash the salt off, pat dry with kitchen paper, then freeze it. Once frozen you can thinly slice the lard and eat it. Try it on some rye bread with Ukrainian honey and chilli vodka, called *horylka*.

This 1980s number was our family's favourite for many years. That is until Uncle Vadik, who had certain fancy connections, bought my mum her first Western cookbook in the mid-1990s (*International Family Favorites* by Ron Kalenuik, which we still use!). Mr Kalenuik's superb French rabbit au vin (with pork belly and mushrooms) had almost irrevocably replaced this old favourite. But we have now decided to bring the 1980s white rabbit back. Don't be alarmed by the amount of garlic – it will mellow and become sweet.

Garlicky white rabbit

Serves 4

80g (3oz) butter
1 rabbit, about 1.25kg (2½lb), jointed
16 small garlic cloves, thinly sliced
250ml (8fl oz) soured cream or crème fraîche
300ml (½ pint) chicken stock or water
2 tablespoons sunflower oil
sea salt flakes
fusilli pasta or rice, to serve

1 Place the butter in the bottom of a heavy-based pan. Keeping 2 thinly sliced garlic cloves behind for a crispy garnish later, add the rabbit pieces and lace with the remaining garlic slices on top.

2 Mix the soured cream and stock or water together and season generously with salt. Pour over the rabbit and bring to boil, then lower the heat and simmer gently for 1½ hours or until the rabbit meat falls off the bone.

3 Heat the sunflower oil in a frying pan and fry the reserved garlic slices until light golden. Be careful not to burn it. Remove and drain on kitchen paper.

4 We love pulling the meat, mixing it with the sauce and serving it with fusilli or rice. Don't forget to sprinkle the crispy garlic on top.

Carp and catfish are a big deal in Ukraine. My dad coaches award-winning fishermen and makes his own bait pellets (called 'The Bomb', ha!), so there is always freshwater fish in the house. There are a few recipes using tomato sauces, soured cream, caramelized onions and honey, and the following has been inspired by those ingredients rather than a particular recipe. Use any seriously meaty fish if you can't find catfish, but I recommend you look for it – it has a unique flavour. I think they feed on crayfish, and I personally love fish that taste of crustaceans (red mullet being my other favourite). *Morkovcha* (Korean Carrots) complement this dish perfectly.

Сом | *Som*
BBQ Catfish

Serves 6

100ml (3½fl oz) dark ale
50g (2oz) clear honey
3 tablespoons soy sauce
625g (1¼lb) catfish, cut into 100g (3½oz) steaks or about 5cm (2 inches) thick
200g (7oz) shallots, sliced
50g (2oz) plain flour
100ml (3½fl oz) sunflower oil, plus extra for oiling
fine sea salt and freshly ground black pepper
Morkovcha (*see* page 88), to serve

1 Mix the ale, honey and soy sauce together in a dish. Add the catfish, cover with clingfilm and leave to marinate in the refrigerator for a couple of hours or overnight.

2 Place the shallot slices and flour in a bowl, add some salt and pepper and mix well.

3 Heat the sunflower oil in a frying pan until hot. Shake the excess flour off the shallots and fry them for about 5–7 minutes until crispy. Remove with a slotted spoon and drain on kitchen paper.

4 Take the fish out of its marinade and pat it dry with kitchen paper. Oil the barbecue rack really well and barbecue the fish for 5 minutes on each side or until cooked through. Serve with the crispy shallots and *Morkovcha* or a garlicky soured cream sauce.

We grew up eating buckets of these. There was always a teenage boy by the side of the road with a fishing rod and a crayfish dangling from it. They are so good that we don't do much to them – they are simply boiled in very well-salted water with loads of dill heads. We then serve them with ice-cold beer. My mum has been known to eat about 60 in one sitting. I don't know what it is about them, but we say they are like sunflower seeds – very easy to eat loads in one go. When my parents were still students, my mum (who didn't know any better) cooked the live crayfish from cold. My dad didn't speak to her after that for two weeks. So make sure you pop the crayfish in the water when it's at a rolling boil; they will die instantly.

Раки | *Raky*

Crayfish

Serves 6 as a beer snack

2.5 litres (4 pints) water
10g (⅓oz) fine sea salt
3 dill heads, or 1 bunch of
   dill stalks
1kg (2lb) live crayfish

1 Bring the water, salt and dill to the boil in a large saucepan. Add the crayfish and cook them for 10–15 minutes.

2 Drain them and serve with beer. Make sure you open the head – a real connoisseur will suck all the goodness out of that.

This is for a real fish lover. During the dodgy 1990s with its racketeering, inflation and general gloom, my beautiful Aunt Lyuda, an artist by trade, couldn't find work, so she moved around villages in a van/portable shop. This was one of her bestsellers (crazy, eh?). Come to Ukraine.

Cured mackerel

Serves 4 as a starter

Stage 1
2 small mackerel
30g (1oz) sea salt flakes
5g (1¼oz) sugar

Stage 2
1 tablespoon sugar
½ teaspoon sea salt flakes
1 large onion, thinly sliced
2 bay leaves, crushed
1 small carrot, peeled and sliced
1 teaspoon black peppercorns
1 tablespoon white wine vinegar

1 Cut the heads and tails off your fish, then gut and wash them, or get your fishmonger to do it. Cut the fish across (bones and all) into steaks 5cm (2 inches) thick.

2 Place the fish in a plastic container, toss in the salt and sugar, seal with the lid and leave to cure in the refrigerator for 24 hours.

3 Next day, wash the salt off the fish, pat dry with kitchen paper and place in a bowl. Add all the remaining ingredients and toss together. Place all of this in a sterilized jar and seal. Keep in the refrigerator and eat the next day.

Соління
Fermented Pickles & Preserves

By sour I mean fermented. We have a wonderful word that describes this kind of brine fermentation – *solinnya*. A little bit of salt, a little bit of warmth and your life is now richer as you have produced the best 'pickles' in the world. We start making this in late autumn (to be eaten in winter), when the right (firmer) types of cabbage become available. Once the cabbage has finished fermenting, it's normally served mixed with thinly sliced red onions and a slick of unrefined sunflower oil. Place some whole cabbage leaves to ferment underneath the sliced cabbage to make *Holubtsi* (*see* page 84).

Квашена капуста | *Kvashena kapusta*
Sour cabbage

Makes a 500ml (17fl oz) jar

500g (1lb) white cabbage, plus 250g (8oz) whole leaves (optional)
150g (5oz) carrots, peeled and roughly grated
40g (1½oz) caster sugar
25g (1oz) fine sea salt

1 Remove the core from the cabbage and shred it into long thin strands. Massage it with your hands to soften and then mix with the carrots.

2 Add the sugar and salt and massage again. If using, place the whole leaves of cabbage at the bottom of a plastic container (or a fermentation barrel if you have one) and pack the sliced cabbage and carrot down tightly.

3 Cover the cabbage with a clean piece of muslin, followed by a plate or a chopping board, then place something really heavy over it to weight it down. Leave in a warm part of your kitchen (25°C/77°F) for about 3 days. Check the cabbage and rinse the muslin cloth every day. When ready, the cabbage will become pleasantly sour.

4 You can then transfer it to a sterilized 500ml (17fl oz) preserving jar and seal. Keep it in the refrigerator, or in a cool cellar like we used to, for a couple of months. The longer you keep it, the sourer it will get – though I think it's nicer when it isn't overly sour.

Whereas the north-west of Ukraine is covered in woodland with beautiful plump ceps and morels, the south of the country is famous for its giant pink tomatoes and aubergines. We used to ferment the last of aubergines to keep us supplied all winter. Ukraine's markets always have a lovely babushka selling these along with a mountain of gherkins and sour cabbage.

Квашені баклажани | *Kvasheni baklazhany*
Sour aubergines

Makesa 1 litre (1¾pint) jar

4 aubergines, about 1kg (2lb) in total
125ml (4fl oz) sunflower oil
400g (13oz) carrots, peeled and roughly grated
1 teaspoon fine sea salt
6 garlic cloves, crushed
8 leaf (or Italian) celery sticks or 4 young celery sticks

1 Place the whole aubergines (stalks and all) in a saucepan, cover with cold water and bring to the boil. Cook for 20 minutes or until they can be easily pierced with a skewer. Drain them, place on a tray, cover with a chopping board weighted down with a heavy object on top and leave overnight to extract as much water as possible.

2 Heat the sunflower oil in a frying pan and sweat the carrots, stirring often, for about 15 minutes until soft but not browned. Let the carrots cool in the oil.

3 Slice off the aubergine stalks, then slice each aubergine in half, starting from the fatter end and almost all the way through but leaving the stalk end whole. Sprinkle ¼ teaspoon of the salt inside each aubergine.

4 Mix the cooled cooked carrots (and their oil) with the crushed garlic, divide it into 4 parts and stuff each aubergine with one part of the mixture. Tie each aubergine with 2 leaf celery 'strings' or a young celery stick and place the stuffed aubergines back on the tray. If you have trouble using the celery 'string' to tie them up, don't worry – just tuck the celery underneath the aubergines for flavour.

5 Cover with clean muslin, weight them down again and leave in a warm place in your kitchen (25°C/77°F) for 2–3 days, making sure to wash or change the muslin each day. The aubergines should acquire a pleasant, mild sourness.

6 Transfer the aubergines to a sterilized 1 litre (1¾ pint) preserving jar and seal. They should then keep unopened in the refrigerator or a cellar all winter.

Picking warm cucumbers from my mum's vegetable patch after a hot summer day is a true pleasure. Sweet and prickly, they are incredible eaten right there and then. When the season comes to its end though, we collect the last few buckets and brine them in our summer kitchen. The flavourings I am giving here are very Ukrainian – not everybody will be able to find sour cherry and horseradish leaves. Simply add whatever you enjoy the taste of: mustard seeds, allspice berries, celery sticks and leaves, red chillies. Sour cherry leaves don't add any flavour, but they are supposed to keep the pickles crisp. Dill is, in my view, essential.

Квашені огірки | *Kvasheni ogirky*
Sour gherkins

Makes 2 x 2 litre (3½ pint) jars

2 litres (3½ pints) water
50g (2oz) fine sea salt
2 bay leaves
3 dill heads or dill
  stalks (fresh or dry)
50g (2oz) horseradish
  leaves or horseradish
  root, chopped
50g (2oz) leaf celery or
  4 thin stalks and leaves
  of regular celery
30g (1oz) blackcurrant
  leaves
4 sour cherry leaves
1 head of garlic, outer
  layer of skin removed
1 long green chilli
  (optional)
10 black peppercorns
1.5kg (3lb) fresh small
  cucumbers

1 Place the water and salt in a saucepan and bring to the boil.

2 Layer all of the flavourings and gherkins or cucumbers in a clean 4 litre (7 pint) container and pour over the hot brine. Place a plate on top and weight it down with something heavy. Leave in a warm place in your kitchen (25°C/77°F) for 3 days.

3 Decant into 2 sterilized 2 litre (3½ pint) preserving jars, seal and keep in the refrigerator. The gherkins should be good to eat after a week or so. They can also be sealed and kept in the refrigerator or a cellar throughout the winter.

When I was a student, my best friend Gabriella and I got really addicted to pickled garlic. Not the worst addiction possible when you are 19, but it was absolute madness, as we ate so much of it that we eventually couldn't bear looking at it for a few years to come. I am ready for a backslide now, since Aunt Nina has given me her Armenian recipe. Beetroot adds a beautiful colour and slight earthiness. This definitely beats the supermarket pickled garlic of my youth.

Armenian pickled wet garlic

**Makes 2 x 1 litre
(1¾ pint) jars**

15 heads of wet (new)
    garlic
1 litre (1¾ pints) water,
    plus 400ml (14fl oz)
    water
3 tablespoons fine sea salt
100g (3½oz) beetroot,
    peeled and sliced
200ml (7fl oz) white wine
    vinegar

1 Soak the unpeeled garlic heads in unsalted water for 3 days, changing the water every day.

2 Drain the garlic and discard the water. Peel off the outer layer of the skin, then place the garlic heads in a plastic container and cover with a plate or chopping board and something heavy to weight it down.

3 Mix the 1 litre (1¾ pints) water and salt together, then pour this brine over the weighted-down garlic. Leave it in your kitchen for 1 week.

4 Drain the garlic. Divide the beetroot slices between 2 sterilized 1 litre (1¾ pint) preserving jars and pop the garlic on top. Mix the vinegar with the 400ml (14fl oz) water and pour this over the garlic. Seal and keep in the refrigerator. It should keep unopened for several months.

My Aunt Nina's grandmother, Liza from Karabakh, used to make this using mountain spring water, and the taste of those pickles was incomparable. Beetroot is often added to Armenian pickles for colour, which is similar to how it is made in the Middle East. These pickles are delicious and we eat them in the summer and in winter. You can buy horseradish leaves and dill stalks in bunches from Polish delis specially for pickling, but if you can't find them or the blackcurrant and cherry leaves, just substitute with some spices or aromatics that you like (celery would be great) or simply leave them out.

Armenian pickles

Makes a 3 litre (5¼ pint) jar

2 beetroots, peeled and sliced into discs
½ small white cabbage, sliced into wedges
200g (7oz) mixed runner beans or French beans, tailed
4 spring onions
1 head of wet (new) garlic, left whole, outer layer peeled
50g (2oz) dill heads or stalks
2 horseradish leaves, or 50g (2oz) fresh horseradish, chopped
2 blackcurrant leaves
2 sour cherry leaves
1 litre (1¾ pints) water
3 tablespoons sea salt flakes
10 black peppercorns

1 Place the beetroot at the bottom of a warm, sterilized 2 litre (3½ pint) preserving jar, then top with the cabbage wedges, beans, spring onions, garlic and all the aromatics, apart from the peppercorns.

2 Bring the water, salt and peppercorns to the boil in a saucepan, then pour over the vegetables. Make sure everything is submerged, then seal and leave in a warm part of your kitchen (25°C/77°F) for about 3 days to pickle, then store in the refrigerator. The beetroot will gradually turn everything a deep pink. It should keep unopened for several months.

These tomatoes must be firm, still green but already starting to ripen. When ready, they will blow your mind and your taste buds when you try them. Embrace the fizziness – they are supposed to be like this. One friend said that they have a quality of a fine burger sauce, and another suggested that slithers could be served with oysters instead of shallots and vinegar. Traditionally, we serve them in winter with hearty, meaty casseroles.

Квашені помідори | *Kvasheni pomidory*
Fermented tomatoes

Makes a 2 x 1 litre
(1¾ pint) jars

35g (1¼oz) fine sea salt
25g (1oz) caster sugar
½ tablespoon allspice
  berries, bruised
½ tablespoon black
  peppercorns
1 litre (1¾pints) water
500g (1lb) Tumbling Tiger
  tomatoes or other
  medium-sized
  flavourful tomatoes
2 dill heads or dill
  stalks (fresh or dry)
1 bay leaf
50g (2oz) celery sticks and
  leaves, chopped

1 Mix the salt, sugar, allspice and peppercorns into the measurement water in a saucepan and bring to the boil. Let the liquid cool down completely and infuse.

2 Place the tomatoes and the other flavourings in a sterilized 2.5 litre (4 pint) preserving jar and pour over the cool infused brine.

3 Seal the jar and leave in a warm place in your kitchen (25°C/77°F) for 1 week until the tomatoes start fermenting. Transfer to the refrigerator or a cellar, where they can be kept unopened all winter.

We rarely use vinegar to pickle anything, but my aunt found this recipe 40 years ago in a Soviet newspaper, and over the years they have lived up to the name that the newspaper gave them, which literally translates as 'tomatoes lick your fingers'. Again, the tomatoes should be firm and undamaged but ripe, and can be kept all winter. You can use any strong oil you like, but a toasty unrefined sunflower oil gives an incredible authentic taste.

Пальчики оближеш | *Pal'chyky oblyzhesh*

Lick-your-fingers tomatoes

**Makes a 2 litre
(3½ pint) jar**

1 litre (1¾ pints) water
30g (1oz) caster sugar
15g (½oz) fine sea salt
2 bay leaves
6 allspice berries
65ml (2½fl oz) white wine
  vinegar
1 tablespoon unrefined
  sunflower oil
500g (1lb) firm but ripe
  pink Bull's Heart or beef
  tomatoes, quartered
5 sprigs of dill, chopped
50g (2oz) leaf celery or
  celery sticks and leaves,
  chopped
3 large garlic cloves,
  chopped
1 onion, sliced

1 Boil the measurement water with the sugar, salt, bay leaves and allspice in a saucepan. Let it cool down completely and infuse, then add the vinegar.

2 Place the sunflower oil, tomato quarters, dill, celery and garlic in a sterilized 2 litre (3½ pint) preserving jar and top with the onion slices.

3 Pour over the cold brine and seal the jar. Leave the tomatoes in a warm place (25°C/77°F) for 10 days and then transfer to the refrigerator or a cellar. These should keep all winter if unopened and stored properly.

Mors is usually associated with a Russian berry drink, but in Ukraine we use it to describe fermented tomato pulp. It's an ancient recipe that was used all winter to make *borshch*. Of course, we can now buy tinned tomatoes, but if you are adventurous, give it a go. It adds an unbelievable kick to winter *borshches* (*see* pages 12–15).

Морс | *Mors*

Fermented tomato passata

Makes a 1 litre (1¾ pint) jar

150g (5oz) fine sea salt
2kg (4lb) large ripe tomatoes (skin discarded), grated
1kg (2lb) whole ripe cherry tomatoes

1 This is simple: mix the salt with the tomato pulp and pour this over the whole cherry tomatoes. Place them in a plastic container with a clean piece of muslin cloth over them and a plate or chopping board on top, then weight them down with something heavy. Leave them in a warm place (25°C/77°F) for 5 days to begin fermenting. It is important that you wash or change the muslin cloth every day. Keep an eye on it every day – you want it to ferment but not to go mouldy.

2 Mash the mixture into a pulp, then transfer to a sterilized 1 litre (1¾ pint) jar, seal and keep in the refrigerator. Once opened, use within 1 month.

Варення
Sweet Conserves

This is my most favourite conserve of all times. It's for those rare quiet afternoons (parents of toddlers would understand) when you sit down in your kitchen for a minute (instead of tidying the house, sod it), read a book or a magazine and lather your toast in butter and this lusciousness. It has a slight but irresistible sour tang and a head-spinning vanilla kick. Who needs chocolate when you have rummy plums? This is ideal as a Christmas gift and is also amazing to use as an alternative to mincemeat in your mince pies.

Plum, rum & raisin conserve

Makes a 450g (¾ pint) jar

100g (3½oz) sultanas
100ml (3½fl oz) rum
200g (7oz) soft dark
  brown sugar
100g (3½oz) good-quality
  clear honey
grated rind and juice of
  1 orange
grated rind and juice of
  1 lemon
100ml (3½fl oz) water
500g (1lb) plums, stoned
  and chopped
1 vanilla pod, slit
  lengthways and the
  seeds scraped out,
  pod reserved

1 Soak the sultanas in the rum overnight.

2 Dilute the sugar, honey and the rind and juice of both the orange and lemon with the measurement water in a heavy-based saucepan and slowly bring everything to the boil.

3 Add the plums, sultanas together with the rum and the vanilla seeds and pod, lower the heat and simmer for 45–60 minutes until thickened.

4 Pour into a warm sterilized 450ml (¾ pint) jar and seal, then let it cool and store in the refrigerator. It should keep unopened for several months.

Сливовое

500г сл
50г щу
300г сахар
300г
мёда
● апельсина
● лимона
50мл рома

● Замочит из
● Смешайте 10
мёд.
● Добавьте ром
примерно час. В

The Kherson region of Ukraine where I am from is watermelon country, and it's where half the country's crop is cultivated (they love the heat). Kris, the photographer, said after seeing them that he could never look at a watermelon in the UK the same way again. During watermelon season in August, there are big trucks by the side of the road full of the huge, firm, stripy beasts. We do unbelievable things to watermelons. We even (yes, you've guessed it) ferment them with salt. Whole. In barrels. I thought that might be too much for an introductory Eastern European cookbook though, so here is some slightly less scary watermelon skin jam – for those who really hate waste and love jams. I add limes to mine, as I like the kick of acidity and bitterness they give, but you can leave them out if you prefer.

Watermelon skin jam

**Makes 2 x 450ml
(¾ pint) jars**

500g (1lb) watermelon
  skin, tough thin green
  rind peeled and
  discarded, white skin
  chopped
300g (10oz) golden caster
  sugar
4 limes, thinly sliced

1 Mix all the ingredients together in a container, cover with clingfilm and leave in the refrigerator overnight.

2 Cook the mixture in a non-reactive saucepan over a low heat, making sure the sugar melts before it boils, for 50 minutes or until the watermelon skin turns translucent.

3 Pour into 2 warm sterilized 450ml (¾ pint) jars, seal and let it cool. Store in the refrigerator. It should keep unopened for several months.

July was the month of head-spinning smells emanating from the summer kitchen. My favourite was when raspberry compote was made. Mum would collect what some may call 'scum' but what I call 'delicious jam foam' and give it to us as a treat – the foaminess is just the air bubbles trapped in sugar syrup after all. Mum used to put a little bit of this jam into my tea when I was ill, and there is nothing more delicious and comforting. You can add some orange rind and juice to the raspberries while they cook if you wish.

Raspberry conserve

Makes a 1 litre (1¾ pint) jar

650g (1lb 5oz) raspberries
300g (10oz) golden caster sugar
a few strips of rind and juice of 1 orange (optional)

1 Place the raspberries, sugar and orange rind and juice, if using, in a heavy-based saucepan and slowly bring to the boil, making sure that the sugar melts before boiling point.

2 Lower the heat and simmer, stirring from time to time, for 45 minutes. This compote will be pretty liquid, but just cook it longer if you prefer a more jammy consistency.

3 Pour into a warm sterilized 1 litre (1¾ pint) jar and seal, then let it cool and store in the refrigerator. Drop a large spoonful into your tea for comfort.

My uncle had a quince tree in his garden and I have always had an overwhelming love for this fruit. We even used to eat it raw (yes, crazy, I know!), or chop it and turn it into jam. I do love it roasted or poached whole though. Add some sea salt flakes and black pepper, remove the vanilla and halve the quantity of sugar to make a delicious addition to roast duck.

Baked quince

Serves 6–8

350ml (12fl oz) water
100g (3½oz) caster sugar
1 vanilla pod, split,
  seeds removed
1 cinnamon stick
2 star anise
5 juniper berries
3–4 quinces, about
  1kg (2lb)

1 Preheat the oven to 160°C/325°F/Gas Mark 3. Place the water with the sugar in a saucepan, add the vanilla seeds and the pod to the pan with the cinnamon stick, star anise and juniper berries and cook over a low heat, stirring regularly, until the sugar dissolves.

2 Cut the quinces in half, then cut in half again lengthways and remove the core. Place the quince quarters in a medium baking dish.

3 Pour the spiced syrup over the quinces. Cover with foil and pop in the oven for 1 hour, then uncover and cook for a further hour or until the quinces are soft and amber coloured.

4 Serve this warm with ice cream, or chilled instead of strawberries for a winter version of the Birthday Ice Cream & Strawberry Cake on page 201.

Mum has an old Ukrainian baking book that she's had since the mid-1970s. It's a treasure of a book and this recipe was an inspiration for her, as she loved making all kinds of conserves for serving with *mlyntsi*: thin Ukrainian crêpes slathered in melted butter. She would literally place a block of butter on a hot pancake while frying the next one. You can use thinly sliced firm apricots instead of strawberries. This conserve will be a little liquid, but I prefer it to really thick, sugary jams.

Gooseberry & strawberry conserve

Makes a 1 litre (1¾ pint) jar

450g (14½oz) gooseberries
350g (11½oz) strawberries
450g (14½oz) golden
  caster sugar

1 Wash the gooseberries and get rid of the stalks. Wash the strawberries, take the green tops off and cut the large ones in half.

2 Place the gooseberries, sugar and a splash of water in a large, heavy-based saucepan and slowly bring to the boil, making sure all the sugar dissolves before it boils. Cook over a very low heat, stirring from time to time, for 1 hour, making sure that the sugar doesn't catch on the base of the pan.

3 Add the strawberries and simmer for another 30 minutes until slightly thickened. Place in a warm sterilized 1 litre (1¾ pint) jar and seal, then let it cool. Store in the refrigerator. It should keep unopened for several months.

My mum declares that this method – involving bringing everything to the boil and letting it cool repeatedly – ensures that the apricots keep their shape, teasing out the pectin gradually without destroying the apricots' good looks. It's not particularly hard – it just requires you to peel yourself off the sofa on a rainy Sunday afternoon every two hours to reboil the jam. You can also crush the stones, remove the kernels, peel them off their brown film and add them to the jam along with a drop of almond essence to make 'tsar's jam'. Watch out when you crush the stones though, as shards will shoot straight at your face.

Apricot jam

Makes a 1 litre (1¾ pint) jar

500g (1lb) apricots, halved and stoned, stones crushed, kernels removed and peeled (optional)
500g (1lb) golden caster sugar
a few strips of rind and juice of 2 lemons
2 drops of almond essence (optional)

1 Place the apricot halves, sugar, peeled apricot kernels, if you are mad enough, lemon rind and juice and almond essence, if using, in a heavy-based saucepan. Slowly bring to the boil, stirring gently but frequently to dissolve the sugar. Simmer the apricots for 10 minutes, then switch off the heat.

2 Let the jam cool, then bring it to the boil again and simmer for 10 minutes.

3 Repeat this cooling and bringing to boil and simmering process twice more until it becomes a jam-like consistency.

4 Pour the conserve into a warm sterilized 1 litre (1¾ pint) jar and seal, then let it cool and store in the refrigerator. Serve on bread or with some lovely Yogurt Drop Scones (see page 183).

It may be hard to find cornel cherries, but I have decided to include this recipe for cultural reference's sake. It may sound strange to leave stones in fruit when making jam, but somehow it never bothered me. The fresh berries are sour and slightly resemble sour plums in flavour.

Cornel cherry jam

**Makes a 1 litre
(1¾ pint) jar**

400g (13oz) cornel
    cherries, stones in
400g (13oz) golden
    granulated sugar
200ml (7fl oz) water

1 Place everything in a saucepan and bring to the boil very slowly, stirring all the time to make sure that the sugar melts before boiling point. Simmer for 1 hour until it thickens.

2 Pour into a warm sterilized 1 litre (1¾ pint) jar, seal and let it cool, then store in the refrigerator. It will keep unopened for several months.

Apart from fruit, vegetables and berries, my grandmother Lusia grew incredible flowers. Peonies, asters, hollyhocks and roses added explosions of juicy colour to her garden. I will never forget the tea roses and their musky, viscous (if I may say that?) aroma. She preserved her summer roses in jars. This is amazing eaten straight from the spoon with a strong cup of black tea with lemon.

Rose petal jam

Makes 4 x 200ml (7fl oz) jars

400g (13oz) unsprayed edible tea rose petals
250ml (8fl oz) water
400g (13oz) granulated sugar
5g (¼oz) citric acid

1 Soak the petals in some cold water for a couple of hours, then drain well.

2 Place the measurement water and sugar in a saucepan and slowly bring to the boil; the sugar needs to dissolve completely before boiling. Add the citric acid and the drained petals, give it all a stir, reduce the heat and simmer for 15 minutes.

3 Pour the jam into 4 warm sterilized 200ml (7fl oz) jars and seal, then let them cool and store in the refrigerator. Enjoy all winter with tea.

My Ukrainian love of all things fruit has manifested itself in this sauce. It's my own recipe and I love it. Do try lemon thyme with this – its floral notes go really beautifully with blackberries. Serve this sauce with *Deruny* (Potato Cakes with Goats' Cheese, *see* page 83) or roast duck or chicken.

Blackberry sauce

Serves 2

25g (1oz) butter
½ tablespoon olive oil
60g (2¼oz) shallots, very
  finely diced
2 teaspoons sherry
  vinegar
40ml (1½fl oz) port
100g (3½oz) blackberries
4 sprigs of lemon thyme,
  leaves picked and
  chopped
1 teaspoon caster sugar
sea salt flakes and freshly
  ground black pepper

1 Heat the butter and olive oil in a frying pan, add the shallots and sherry vinegar and sweat over a low heat for 10 minutes until the shallots have softened.

2 Raise the heat to medium. Now watch your eyebrows and shout 'flambé!' as you add the port, tilt the pan away from you to catch the flames and flambé until the flame dies down. It may not do much in terms of flavour (it just burns the alcohol off more quickly), but it may impress your date.

3 Add the blackberries, crush them slightly with a fork and cook over a medium–low heat for about 5 minutes. Add the lemon thyme and sugar, season well with salt and pepper and cook for another minute or so.

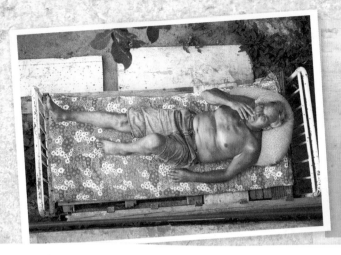

Десерти
Desserts

Please do use butter here instead of margarine if the latter screams 1980s credit crunch to you too much. In Soviet Ukraine there was a perpetual credit crunch, so we got used to using margarine. Besides, the cheese here adds enough richness, so butter may be a slight overkill. Be careful though – whatever type of fat you use, you may not be able to stop eating these.

Берлінське печиво | *Berlins'ke pechyvo*

Berlin curd cheese biscuits

Makes 20–22

80g (3oz) margarine
200g (7oz) *Syr* (*see* page
   109) or Polish *twaróg*
200g (7oz) plain flour,
   plus extra for dusting
1 teaspoon baking powder
50g (2oz) granulated
   sugar

1 Mix the margarine and cheese together in a bowl until well combined. Sift the flour and baking powder together and then mix it into the cheese mixture.

2 Knead the dough briefly, wrap in clingfilm and chill in the refrigerator for at least 30 minutes if you have the time.

3 Preheat the oven to 180°C/350°F/Gas Mark 4. Line a large baking sheet with silicone paper.

4 Flour the work surface well and then roll the dough out into a sheet a bit less than 2mm (about ⅛ inch) thick. Stamp out 10cm (4 inch) circles with a glass or a cookie cutter, then re-roll the offcuts to make more.

5 Pour the sugar into a shallow plate. Now dip one side of a dough circle into the sugar, then fold the circle in half, sugar side in. Dip one side of the semicircle in sugar and again fold in half, sugar side in. Finally, dip one side of the folded semicircle in sugar and place on the lined baking sheet sugar side up. Repeat with the rest of the dough circles.

6 If your kitchen is warm and the dough feels soft, chill the biscuits in the refrigerator for 20 minutes, then pop them in the oven and bake for about 30–40 minutes or until they are deep golden all over.

This is more of a breakfast and is one of my most favourite recipes of all time – I make it for my son very often as my mum did for me. They are perfect served with some yogurt and Gooseberry & Strawberry Conserve (*see* page 171) or Apricot Jam (*see* page 172).

Оладки | *Oladky*
Yogurt drop scones

Makes 10

160ml (5½fl oz) natural
  yogurt or *kefir*
1 egg, lightly beaten with
  a pinch of sea salt flakes
90–100g (3¼–3½oz) plain
  flour
½ teaspoon bicarbonate
  of soda
pinch of fine sea salt
2 tablespoons sunflower
  oil
natural yogurt and
  conserve or jam,
  to serve

1 Mix all the ingredients except the sunflower oil together well in a bowl with a fork. The batter should be of a soft dropping consistency.

2 Brush a frying pan lightly with the oil over a medium heat, then drop separate large tablespoonfuls of batter into the pan and cook for 2 minutes on each side. Repeat with the remaining batter and add more oil if necessary. Serve warm with Greek yogurt and conserve or jam.

These dry biscuits are beyond moreish – there is nothing better than one (or ten) of these with some coffee. Some of the ground nuts are mixed into the dough, making for a great texture and flavour. My mum normally uses walnuts, but for me there isn't a nut to beat a pecan. You can also use pistachios – they will add an incredible colour.

Сухарики | *Sukharyky*
Ukrainian biscotti

Makes about 40

150g (5oz) pecan nuts or walnut halves
1 egg yolk
60g (2¼oz) caster sugar
75g (3oz) butter, softened
1 tablespoon rum (optional)
pinch of fine sea salt
50g (2oz) sultanas or ready-to-eat dried apricots, chopped
150g (5oz) plain flour, plus extra for dusting
½ tablespoon milk, to glaze

1 Line a baking sheet with silicone paper and set aside. Blitz half the nuts in a food processor until finely ground. Cut the rest of the nuts in half lengthways and set aside.

2 Mix the egg yolk, sugar, butter, rum (if using), blitzed nuts and salt together in a bowl, then mix in the dried fruit and flour. Knead the mixture in the bowl briefly – you should end up with a soft dough.

3 Flour your work surface lightly, divide the dough into 4 pieces and roll each piece into sausage shapes, 2.5cm (1 inch) in diameter. Flatten them slightly, then brush the tops with the milk. Arrange the reserved nuts vertically, side by side (like little soldiers), along the tops of each sausage. Push the nuts down ever so slightly to make sure they don't fall off. Carefully transfer the sausages to the prepared baking sheet, then chill in the refrigerator for 30–60 minutes.

4 Preheat the oven to 180°C/350°F/Gas Mark 4. Bake the sausage shapes for 15 minutes, then remove from the oven and carefully (don't burn your fingers) slice each sausage into 10–12 pieces. Lower the oven temperature to 150°C/300°F/Gas Mark 2 and bake the biscotti for a further 30 minutes, then switch the oven off and leave the biscotti inside to dry and cool. They will become crispy as they cool (but not hard), buttery and nutty – an ace addition to a morning coffee.

This is a Russian version of the French millefeuille. Some say Russians ate this to celebrate Napoleon's demise, cutting the cake into sinister triangular pieces. Either way, it is definitely a celebratory dish – there isn't a New Year or a birthday without this cake, and given the size of my extended family, we make two at a time. Some folk put nuts in it, but to me it's perfect the way it is. My mum prefers it as soon as the cream has been spread over the pastry so that it's still crispy, but I leave it in the refrigerator overnight, letting the pastry absorb all of the crème pât. For me, the pastry is ideal scaffolding material for a giant custard tower.

Наполеон | *Napoleon*

Napoleon cake

Serves 10

Pastry

250g (8oz) margarine, chilled in the freezer

550g (1lb 2oz) plain flour, plus extra for dusting

125ml (4fl oz) cold water

1 tablespoon white wine vinegar

Crème pâtissière

1 litre (1¾ pints) milk

2 vanilla pods, slit lengthways and the seeds scraped out, pods reserved

7 egg yolks

200g (7oz) caster sugar

75g (3oz) plain flour

50g (2oz) butter, cubed

1 Place the frozen margarine in the flour in a bowl and cut it into the flour with a knife or rub in with your fingertips to make 'breadcrumbs'.

2 Mix the water with the vinegar and add to the flour. Knead into a firm dough, wrap in clingfilm and chill in the refrigerator for at least 3 hours, but preferably overnight.

3 Preheat the oven to 200°C/400°F/Gas Mark 6. Flour the work surface and roll the pastry into a sausage shape. Cut into 12 pieces and roll each piece out, one by one, as thinly as you can into a 22cm (8½ inch) diameter disc. Pop each sheet (in turn) on to a dry baking sheet and bake for 4–5 minutes or until pale golden and puffed up in places. Watch it, as the pastry will quickly burn! When all the pastry discs are done, set them aside on a wire rack to cool. The first pastry sheet will have coloured more than the others, so once cool, crumble it and keep for decoration.

4 To make the crème pâtissière, heat the milk and the scraped vanilla seeds and pods in a large saucepan. Meanwhile, whisk the egg yolks with the sugar and the flour in a bowl. When the milk is near boiling point, quickly tip some of it into the egg mixture, stirring it vigorously so that the eggs don't scramble. Tip the egg mixture into the rest of the milk and cook over a medium-low heat, stirring constantly, for about 10–15 minutes or until the cream thickens to a custard-like consistency. Add the butter, a piece at a time, and stir until combined. Let it cool a little, then cover with a piece of clingfilm to stop a skin from forming and let it cool completely.

5 Spread the crème pât over each pastry sheet, layering them up and popping the pastry bubbles as you go. This way, the pastry cream will fill the craters where the bubbles have popped and won't leak out.

6 Sprinkle the crumbled pastry on top and place the cake in the refrigerator for the pastry to absorb the cream, or eat straight away if you are strange like my mum. The next day, I trim away the dry edges that managed to escape the crème pâtissière's engulfment.

We normally boil these where I come from, but I much prefer this steamed recipe from Poltava (central Ukraine), which I started using a few years ago. These are also superb with fresh sour cherries, blackberries or apricots.

Вареники з полуницею | *Varenyky z polunytseyu*

Steamed pasta with strawberries

Makes 25 dumplings

1 teaspoon sugar
pinch of fine sea salt
10g (⅓oz) fresh yeast
125ml (4fl oz) warm water
½ teaspoon sunflower oil,
   plus extra for oiling
225g (7½oz) plain flour,
   plus extra for dusting
½ teaspoon bicarbonate
   of soda
250g (8oz) small
   strawberries, hulled and
   cut into quarters
maple syrup or clear
   honey, to serve

1 Work the sugar and salt into the yeast with a fork in a bowl, helping it to dissolve, then add the warm (but not too warm) measurement water and the sunflower oil and leave for 15 minutes to let the yeast activate.

2 Sift the flour and bicarbonate of soda together and add it to the yeast mixture gradually, mixing with a spoon.

3 Dust your work surface generously and work the dough as you would pasta dough to bring it together. It should be firm and elastic.

4 Divide the dough into 2 pieces and roll out each piece as thinly as you can (a bit less than 2mm/about ⅛ inch thick is perfect). Stamp out circles about 8cm (3¼ inches) in diameter with a glass or a cookie cutter. You can re-roll the offcuts if they are not too dry and cut out more circles.

5 Place 2 or 3 strawberry quarters inside each dough circle. Bring both sides of the circle up and pinch them firmly together, making sure no air is left inside the dumpling.

6 Oil a steamer (or colander set over a saucepan of boiling water) and pop the *varenyky* inside. Cover and steam for 5 minutes.

7 Drizzle with maple syrup or honey and serve immediately. Be careful though, as the strawberries inside will be piping hot.

I've always loved the name of these, and there has always been something dangerously attractive about the whole wasp element of this dish. Also, these buns looked very much like the stuff we'd see in foreign films. Were there Swedish cinnamon rolls in Ingmar Bergman films? Maybe not. Were they in the incredibly popular Astred Lindgren Karlsson-on-the-Roof cartoon adaptations? The Moomins?! Either way, they looked exotic and fed my fantasies of living somewhere abroad when it was still a risky and unrealistic thought.

Осине гніздо | *Osyne gnizdo*

Wasp nest buns

Makes 15–20

50g (2oz) butter, softened, plus extra for greasing
2 tablespoons caster sugar
pinch of fine sea salt
1 teaspoon vanilla extract
15g (½oz) fresh yeast
2 egg yolks
250ml (8fl oz) warm milk
500g (1lb) plain flour, plus extra for dusting
100g (3½oz) granulated sugar
50g (2oz) pecan nuts, crushed

1 Preheat the oven to 180°C/350°F/Gas Mark 4, and butter a 24cm (9½ inch) round cake tin.

2 Work the caster sugar, salt and vanilla extract into the yeast with a fork in a bowl, helping the yeast to dissolve. Add the egg yolks and work these in to form a paste.

3 Add the milk (make sure it's only slightly warm, otherwise the yeast will die), sift in the flour and mix it into a soft dough.

4 Generously flour the work surface and knead the dough briefly. Make sure the surface is well floured and then roll the dough out as thinly as you can.

5 Brush the dough with the softened butter (I just use my hand), then evenly sprinkle over the granulated sugar, followed by the crushed nuts.

6 Roll up the sheet to create a long sausage, then cut it across into 15–20 pieces. Don't worry if you have some baby ones, they'll add to the charm.

7 Arrange them pretty side up in a haphazard manner in the greased cake tin. Bake for about 30–40 minutes, making sure you don't open the oven door prematurely. The buns should be plump and golden and dangerously inviting.

There isn't a cheesecake more delicious and easier to make than this. Not too sweet, but silky inside with a delicious caramelized crust on top, this is a rare dessert where I actually enjoy raisins. You can of course leave them out or add some chopped dried apricots instead. Semolina adds a subtle texture. I've also used maize flour instead of regular wheat flour here for a gluten-intolerant friend and you couldn't tell the difference!

Запіканка | *Zapinkanka*
Baked Ukrainian cheesecake

Serves 6

100g (3½oz) butter, melted and cooled, plus extra for greasing
500g (1lb) *Syr* (*see* page 109) or good-quality Polish *twaróg*, or cottage cheese
3 eggs
100g (3½oz) granulated sugar
100g (3½oz) semolina
100g (3½oz) plain flour or yellow cornmeal flour
1 teaspoon vanilla extract
2 tablespoons raisins or sultanas
Gooseberry & Strawberry Conserve (*see* page 171)

1 Preheat the oven to 160°C/325°F/Gas Mark 3, and brush a 1kg (2lb) loaf tin with melted butter to grease.

2 Mix all the ingredients together in a bowl and let the mixture stand for 15 minutes to allow the semolina to absorb a bit of the moisture.

3 Pour the cake batter into the greased tin and bake for 1 hour or until the cake is firm and forms a golden crust on top. Let it cool in the tin for 15 minutes, then turn out. Serve it warm or at room temperature as it is or with a dollop of Gooseberry & Strawberry Conserve.

This is one of the easiest cakes to whip up in seconds. Whenever we had a craving for something sweet, my mum would make this, which she simply called *biskvit* ('a sponge'). It is mostly apples, combined with some fluffy eggy batter spiced with cinnamon and sprinkled with icing sugar.

Бісквіт | *Biskvit*

Apple sponge

Serves 6

butter, for greasing
5 eggs
200g (7oz) caster sugar
200g (7oz) plain flour,
  sifted
1 teaspoon ground
  cinnamon
4 green apples, cored and
  thinly sliced
icing sugar, for dusting

1 Preheat the oven to 180°C/350°F/Gas Mark 4, and butter a 20 x 30cm (8 x 12 inch) cake tin with a removable base.

2 Beat the eggs and caster sugar together in a bowl with an electric whisk for at least 5 minutes until very thick, pale and foamy. There is no raising agent in this cake, so the amount of air you beat into it is essential.

3 Gently fold the flour into the egg mixture.

4 Mix the cinnamon with the apples, then tip the apples into the prepared cake tin and pour the cake batter evenly over the apples. Bake for 35 minutes or until a skewer inserted into the cake comes out clean.

5 Let it cool in the tin. Dust with some icing sugar, cut into squares and serve.

This is for honey lovers who are not scared of weird cake-making methods. You can use a good-quality crème fraîche to make the icing, but what you are looking for here is a beautiful balance between slightly sour and honeycomb sweet.

Медовик | *Medovyk*

Honey cake

Serves 8–10

200g (7oz) butter, cubed and chilled, plus extra for greasing
2 eggs, lightly beaten
200g (7oz) golden caster sugar
200ml (7fl oz) clear honey
1 teaspoon bicarbonate of soda
1 tablespoon white wine vinegar
300g (10oz) plain flour
150–200g (5–7oz) pecans, half left whole, the rest toasted and roughly crushed

Cream
500ml (7fl oz) soured cream
100g (3½oz) golden caster sugar
grated zest and juice of ½ lemon

1 Preheat the oven to 180°C/350°F/Gas Mark 4, and lightly butter 4 x 24cm (9½ inch) cake tins (or use 2 in batches).

2 Mix the eggs, butter, sugar and honey together in a large heatproof bowl and place it over a small saucepan of simmering water. Give it a stir, to help the butter to melt, then whisk with an electric whisk until the mixture becomes warm and fluffy. Let it cool.

3 Place the bicarbonate of soda in a cup and pour the vinegar over the soda, then tip the foaming mixture into the honey mixture and give it a vigorous stir.

4 Gradually fold in the flour to form a thick but fluid batter.

5 Spoon one-quarter of the mixture into each prepared cake tin and bake for 15 minutes or until deep golden. The sponges will still be soft while warm, so let them cool before taking them out of their tins.

6 For the cream, put the soured cream into a large bowl and whisk with an electric whisk. Add the sugar and whisk some more, then add the lemon zest and juice and whisk again until the cream is fluffy. Use half the cream to sandwich the 4 sponge layers together, then use the remaining cream to cover the top and sides.

7 Decorate the sides with the crushed nuts. Use the pecan halves to decorate the top of the cake. Alternatively, crush all the nuts and sprinkle them evenly all over.

We just call this 'the ice cream cake'. I think my mum found this recipe in a Soviet newspaper in the mid-1980s and she's made it for my birthday every year without fail. Ice cream choices in the USSR were stark, but there was *plombir* (the Russians' copy of the French *plombière*). It was so, so deliciously milky – in my memory it was like the best *fior di latte* that I have since tried in Italy, but better. They still make it, but it's not the same. Or we are not the same. Either way, blisteringly hot meringue, cold ice cream and fragrant strawberries from our garden with a lovely eggy sponge absorbing it all is one of my brightest childhood memories.

Birthday ice cream & strawberry cake

Serves 10

Sponge
butter, for greasing
5 eggs
200g (7oz) caster sugar
200g (7oz) plain flour

Filling
500g (1lb) good-quality
   fior di latte gelato or
   vanilla ice cream
500g (1lb) strawberries,
   hulled and sliced
   lengthways

Meringue
4 egg whites
100g (3½oz) caster sugar

1 Preheat the oven to 180°C/350°F/Gas Mark 4. Grease a 22cm (8½ inch) round cake tin with a removable base, or line it with baking parchment if you can be bothered.

2 To make the sponge, beat the eggs and sugar together in a bowl with an electric whisk for at least 5 minutes until very thick, pale and foamy. There is no raising agent in this cake, so the amount of air you beat into it is essential. Gently fold in the flour.

3 Pour the cake batter into the prepped tin and bake for 30–35 minutes. Let it cool in the tin for 10 minutes, then remove and cool completely on a wire rack. Carefully slice in half horizontally.

4 Take the ice cream for the filling out of the freezer to soften slightly. Meanwhile, whisk the egg whites with the sugar in a large, clean bowl until stiff. Preheat your grill to high.

5 Now you have to move quickly. Cover the bottom layer of sponge with half the ice cream and half the strawberries, then cover with the other sponge layer and top with the remaining ice cream, followed by the remaining strawberries. Spread the meringue over and pop it under the grill. Don't leave it unattended for a moment – it should only take 30 seconds– 1 minute to turn golden brown. Serve immediately.

Just when you thought these recipes may become a little less nuts I give you meringues baked with sweetened noodles. The Russian translation of this crazy dessert (found by my sister-in-law in a 1970s Soviet cookery book) is called (rather naffly) 'capricious lady'. Sis-in-law won me over with this and I worked hard to recreate that seductive texture and crunch, as with time this recipe has been forgotten and replaced by panna cottas and tiramisus. I am bringing it back. Give it a go – it will change your perception of meringues forever.

Дамський каприз | *Dams'kyy kapryz*
Nutty noodle meringues

Makes 8

Dough
2 egg yolks
2 teaspoons caster sugar
2 teaspoons sunflower oil
100g (3½oz) plain flour,
   plus extra for dusting

Meringue
2 egg whites
75g (3oz) caster sugar
75g (3oz) soft light brown
   sugar
200g (7oz) pecan nuts,
   walnuts or pistachio
   nuts, roughly chopped

1 To make the dough, place the egg yolks, sugar and oil in a large bowl and mix together with a fork. Gradually add the flour, mixing everything into a firm, pasta-like dough. Knead it briefly and leave it to rest at room temperature for 15 minutes.

2 Preheat the oven to 150°C/300°F/Gas Mark 2, and line a large baking sheet with baking parchment.

3 Dust your work surface with flour and roll out the dough into a 20cm (8 inch) square sheet. Roll it into a tube and slice across as thinly as it is humanly possible. Untangle the sliced noodles with your fingers and place on the prepared baking sheet. Bake for 10 minutes or until they are dry and golden.

4 Lower the oven temperature to 120°C/250°F/Gas Mark ½. Line the baking sheet with new baking parchment.

5 Whisk the egg whites and both sugars in a large, grease-free bowl until stiff, then gently mix in the noodles and chopped nuts. Don't be alarmed if it doesn't look like there is enough meringue – the meringue acts as a binding agent here, so it should mostly be noodles and nuts.

6 Place 8 separate spoonfuls of the noodle meringue on the lined baking sheet and bake for 1 hour until golden and crisp.

Encased in warm, pillowy dough, the grated, sugared pumpkin melts into an incredible sweet paste in this version of *plachindy* – my mum's childhood autumnal treat that never lost its appeal, usually served with a little bit of soured cream. I now make it for my son and nephews and they love it. One of them hates pumpkin, but he would have never guessed that's what the 'delicious sweet cream' inside the flatbreads is made from! I usually serve them with some Greek yogurt, as the warm sweetness of the filling against the coolness of the yogurt is a winning combination.

Плачінди з гарбузом | *Plachindy z garbuzom*
Moldovan pumpkin breads

Makes 4

500g (1lb) pumpkin or butternut squash, peeled, deseeded and grated using the large holes of a box grater
250g (8oz) golden caster sugar
½ recipe quantity of *Kefir* Dough (*see* page 48)
plain flour, for dusting
2 tablespoons sunflower oil
Greek yogurt, to serve

1 Mix the grated pumpkin or squash and sugar together in a bowl and let it stand while you make the dough.

2 Divide the dough into 4 pieces. Flour the work surface really well and roll out each piece of dough, one by one, into a 20cm (8 inch) diameter circle.

3 Spread some of the pumpkin or squash mixture on to each dough circle, then follow steps 4–7 on page 47 to finish preparing the flatbread.

4 Fry the breads in the sunflower oil, or brush them with oil and cook them under your grill for a different but still delicious result. Serve with Greek yogurt.

Despite the name, this cake has very little to do with Prague. Originally dreamed up by a prominent Soviet patisserie developer, his recipe was even more elaborate than the one I am giving here, involving three types of cream and four types of alcohol! This is a sumptuous dessert – a little bit with coffee is perfect.

Празький торт | *Praz'kyy tort*

Prague cake

Serves 10

Sponge
5 eggs, fresh and cold
150g (5oz) caster sugar
80g (3oz) butter, melted and cooled, plus extra for greasing (optional)
175g (6oz) flour
30g (1oz) cocoa powder

Drizzle
5 tablespoons caster sugar
50ml (2fl oz) Cognac
1 tablespoon water

Filling
4 egg yolks
4 tablespoons water
1 tablespoon cocoa powder
200g (7oz) slightly salted butter, softened
240g (7¾oz) condensed milk

1 Place a medium metal bowl in the freezer, for making the filling later on.

2 Preheat the oven to 180°C/350°F/Gas Mark 4, and prep a 23cm (9 inch) round springform cake tin with a removable base by buttering it or lining it with baking parchment.

3 For the sponge, beat the eggs and sugar together in a bowl with an electric whisk for at least 5 minutes until very thick, pale and foamy. Trickle in the melted butter. Sift the flour and cocoa together and then gently fold into the batter with a spatula. Try not to knock any air out of the sponge – there is no raising agent, so air is all you've got to help it rise.

4 Pour the cake batter gently into the prepared tin and bake for 25 minutes. Test it by gently touching the top with your finger – it should spring right back. Switch the oven off and leave the cake in the oven but with the door open.

5 Once the cake is cool, open the tin but not completely. To cut the cake into 3 equal discs, do the following: place the base of the tin on something stable and tall (like a large jar) and push the cake out by two-thirds, then slice it in half horizontally with a bread knife. Push the cake up out of the tin a little more and cut across the cake again, making sure that the next disc is the same thickness as the first. You should end up with 3 discs of the same thickness.

Continued overleaf

Continued from previous page

Ganache

300g (10oz) plain dark
   chocolate (70% cocoa
   solids), finely chopped
75g (3oz) butter

edible flowers, to decorate
   (optional)

6 To make the drizzle, heat the sugar, Cognac and measurement water in a small saucepan and boil briefly, then let it cool and drizzle over the sponges.

7 Next, make the filling by heating the egg yolks and measurement water in a glass bowl set over a pan of simmering water, whisking constantly until the mixture turns thick and foamy. Stir in the cocoa powder and take off the heat.

8 Take the metal bowl out of the freezer and place the softened butter in it, then beat it with an electric whisk. When it's starting to foam, trickle in the condensed milk, then gently fold in the cooled yolk mixture.

9 To make the ganache, pop the chocolate and butter into a glass bowl and set it over a pan of simmering water. Let it melt slowly, then give it a gentle stir once it looks almost melted – don't disturb it too much or it will go grainy.

10 Meanwhile, use the filling to sandwich the 3 sponge layers together, then spread the chocolate ganache on the top and down the sides of the cake. I like to decorate my Prague cake with a light sprinkling of edible flowers before serving – just for kicks.

This morbid-sounding recipe is Russian. I always try to think of the painting *Ophelia* by Sir John Everett Millais when I make it. They used to use thick hessian sacks to drown the dough in, but you can always just put the dough in the refrigerator instead.

Утопленик | *Utoplenyk*

Floater dough

Makes 600g (1lb 5oz)

25g (1oz) caster sugar
1 large egg yolk
½ teaspoon vanilla extract
15g (½oz) fresh yeast
   or 7g (¼oz) dried active
   yeast
125ml (4fl oz) warm milk
125g (4oz) margarine,
   melted
350g (12oz) plain flour,
   plus extra for dusting

1 Work the sugar, egg yolk and vanilla extract into the yeast with a fork in a bowl, helping it to dissolve. Add the warm (but not hot!) milk and the melted margarine.

2 Gradually add the flour and work the mixture into a soft dough.

3 Knead the dough on a floured work surface until it stops sticking to your hands.

4 Pop it into a plastic bag that you can seal really well and place it into a large container filled with cold water. When the dough floats to the top, it's ready. Alternatively, put it in the refrigerator for a couple of hours, allowing it to slowly double in size.

The sight of a crimson poppy field is almost as common as the glistening gold of sunflowers in Ukraine. Both my grandmother Vera and my Aunt Zhenia made incredible poppy seed rolls. And it is something my mother would post to my brother in a cardboard box when he was a student at university in Odessa. This would go alongside other goodies such as *tushonka* (a type of pork rillettes) and a huge fresh duck, which would be clumsily roasted by my brother Sasha and cousin Bogdan and eaten in one sitting while playing Nintendo's Duck Hunt (instead of studying). Yep, busted!

Рулет з маком | *Rulet z makom*

Poppy seed roll

Serves 8–10

150g (5oz) poppy seeds
250ml (8fl oz) hot milk
100g (3½oz) butter,
  softened, plus extra
  for greasing
150g (5oz) caster sugar
1 teaspoon vanilla extract,
  or 1 vanilla pod, slit
  lengthways and seeds
  scraped out
200g (7oz) pecan nuts or
  walnuts, roughly
  chopped
1 recipe quantity of
  Floater Dough (*see*
  page 209)
beaten egg, to glaze

1 Soak the poppy seeds in the hot milk for 1 hour or longer.

2 Preheat the oven to 180°C/350°F/Gas Mark 4, and prep a baking sheet by lightly greasing it with butter.

3 Drain the poppy seeds in a fine sieve and then bash with the sugar, in batches, using a pestle and mortar.

4 Mix the sugary poppy seeds with the softened butter, vanilla extract or seeds and nuts.

5 Roll the Floater Dough out into a rectangle 40 x 30cm (15¾ x 12 inches). Spread the poppy seed mixture over the dough evenly, leaving a 1cm (½ inch) border all around the edges. Roll it up as tightly as you can. Brush the roll generously with egg wash and place on the greased baking sheet.

6 Bake for 45 minutes or until cooked through.

This is ultimate childhood comfort nostalgia food – my mum would make these for breakfast. The best bit was always the sugary soured cream sauce. I now add maple syrup instead and it works a treat.

Сирники | *Syrnyky*

Curd cheese patties in maple sauce

Makes 8

250g (8oz) *Syr* (*see* page 109) or Polish *twaróg*
pinch of fine sea salt
1 tablespoon caster sugar
1 egg, lightly beaten
50–80g (2–3oz) plain flour
1 tablespoon sunflower oil
250g (8oz) soured cream
1 vanilla pod, slit lengthways and seeds scraped out
60g (2¼oz) maple syrup or clear honey

1 Mix the cheese, salt, sugar and egg together thoroughly in a bowl, adding enough flour to create a soft and slightly sticky dough.

2 Form the dough into 8 patties 5cm (2 inches) in diameter and 2cm (¾ inch) thick.

3 Heat the oil in a frying pan and brown the patties on both sides, then layer them in a heavy-based saucepan.

4 Mix the soured cream with the vanilla seeds and maple syrup or honey and pour over the patties. Bring to the boil and simmer over a low heat for 7–10 minutes. We eat this for breakfast or as a dessert and it's good warm or cold.

Now that I live in the UK, I find it near impossible to buy fresh sour cherries. Not even frozen. I hear that you can go to pick-your-own farms in the summer, so if they don't hit my local farmers' market next year, I will make sure to go and pick loads, as there is nothing like them. We grow and use them extensively in Ukraine, where they just drop off trees in the streets in June. If you have the same trouble with sourcing the sour sort, try macerating regular cherries in some pomegranate molasses or lemon juice to add a sour note. The pastry is not like a tart – be prepared for some pillowy, brioche breadiness instead.

Apricot & sour cherry pie

Serves 8

200g (7oz) fresh sour cherries or regular cherries
3 tablespoons pomegranate molasses or lemon juice, if using regular cherries
butter, for greasing
500g (1lb) apricots, halved, stoned
200g (7oz) granulated sugar
1 recipe quantity of Floater Dough (*see* page 209)
1 egg, lightly beaten
100g (3½oz) ground almonds

1 Halve the cherries and remove the stones. If using regular cherries, macerate them in the pomegranate molasses or lemon juice for a couple of hours.

2 Preheat the oven to 180°C/350°F/Gas Mark 4, and lightly butter a 24cm (9½ inch) round cake tin or pie dish.

3 Drain the the sour cherries or the regular cherries and mix with the apricot halves and sugar.

4 Pinch one-fifth of the Floater Dough off and set aside. Roll the rest out into a circle 10cm (4 inches) larger than the diameter of your cake tin or dish. Place the circle inside the greased tin or dish, making sure that the dough goes up the sides as well. Cut the reserved dough into long strips for making a lattice for the top of the pie.

5 Brush the base of the pastry case with some of the beaten egg and sprinkle with ground almonds – this should prevent the pie going soggy when it cools. Add the fruit filling and arrange the lattice bits over the top. Brush the lattice with the remaining beaten egg and bake for 55 minutes or until it turns deep dark golden.

These are Ukrainian 'angel wing' pastry crisps. Originally, they used to be fried in lard (think of Portuguese *pastel de nata* lard pastry). I add some ground black cardamom seeds to the sugar, but feel free to use vanilla sugar instead.

Ukrainian fried pastries with black cardamom

Makes 40 pastries

250g (8oz) plain flour, plus extra for dusting
pinch of bicarbonate of soda
50g (2oz) butter, cubed and chilled
1 egg
1 egg yolk
25g (1oz) caster sugar
1 tablespoon white wine vinegar
50g (2oz) soured cream
1 tablespoon vodka
pinch of salt
250ml (8fl oz) sunflower oil
50g (2oz) icing sugar, sifted
5 black cardamom pods, crushed and seeds extracted, then ground into a powder
dulce de leche or chocolate sauce, to serve

1 To make the dough, mix the flour and bicarbonate of soda together, then rub in the butter with your fingertips until well combined.

2 Make a well in the centre of the flour mixture and pour in the egg, egg yolk, sugar, vinegar, soured cream, vodka and salt, then mix well into a firm pastry dough.

3 Flour your work surface really well and divide the dough into 2 pieces. Roll one piece of dough out as thinly as you can. Slice the dough into 4cm (1½ inch) strips and then diagonally across so that you end up with 20 diamonds. Make a 3cm (1¼ inch) slash in the centre of each diamond and pull one of the ends through the slash. Repeat with the second piece of dough.

4 Heat the sunflower oil in a medium saucepan until very hot – be very careful with hot oil, placing it at the back of the hob if you have kids or crazy pets. Line a large plate with some kitchen paper.

5 Drop the diamonds in carefully and fry them briefly until they float to the surface. Lift them out with a slotted spoon and drain them on the kitchen paper.

6 Mix the icing sugar with the cardamom and sprinkle over the pastries. I also like to treat these as nicely as I treat churros, dipping them into dulce de leche or chocolate sauce before devouring.

Sometimes called *kulich* but we call it *paska* in the south, this is a slightly bonkers cousin of the Italian panettone. Don't be put off by the mashed potato starter – it adds a beautiful texture to the bread. When my friend Emma tested the original recipe, I received an alarmed email from her that simply enquired, 'Is your Aunt a professional baker?' There was so much dough and it was so alive that it exploded in her huge Magimix bowl and all over the refrigerator. Moral of the story – we make A LOT of these during Easter, which is our biggest religious holiday.

Паска | *Paska*
Ukrainian Easter bread

Makes 3 x 800g (1lb 10oz) breads

Starter
3 potatoes, peeled and chopped
1 litre (1¾ pints) cold water
3 tablespoons organic plain flour

Dough
250ml (8fl oz) warm milk
15g (¾oz) fresh yeast or 7g (¼oz) dried active yeast
4 egg yolks, at room temperature
150g (5oz) caster sugar
1kg (2lb) plain flour
sunflower oil, for oiling
100g (3½oz) sultanas

Glaze
175g (6oz) icing sugar
2 teaspoons vanilla extract
2 tablespoons water
hundreds and thousands, to decorate (optional)

1 For the starter, place the potatoes in a saucepan, cover with the water and bring to the boil. Cook for 15 minutes or until quite soft.

2 Pour away all but 200ml (7fl oz) of the cooking water and mash the potatoes with the remaining liquid.

3 Add the flour and mix well, then cover and leave in a warm place for 12 hours.

4 To make the dough, add the milk (make sure it's warm but not hot) and the yeast to the starter and mix well.

5 Beat the egg yolks with the sugar in a large bowl with an electric whisk until foamy.

6 Fold the milk and yeast mixture into the egg mixture. Gradually sift in and mix in the flour – the dough should be firm but bouncy. Cover the dough with a clean tea towel and leave to rise in a warm place for about an hour.

7 Moisten your hands with some sunflower oil and knead the dough for about 15 minutes. Scatter the sultanas on your work surface and knead them into the dough.

8 Now divide the dough into 4 pieces. Oil 3 x 800g (1lb 10oz) cleaned tomato cans and half-fill them with the dough. Leave to prove in a warm place for 1 hour.

9 Meanwhile, preheat the oven to 180°C/350°F/Gas Mark 4.

10 Place the cans on a baking sheet and bake for 40–45 minutes on the lowest shelf of the oven. Let the breads cool completely in the tins, then run a palette knife around the edges to help remove from the tins.

11 To make the glaze, whisk the icing sugar, vanilla extract and water together in a bowl, then brush over the top of the breads, letting it drip along the sides. Decorate with hundreds and thousands, if you like.

Напої
Drinks

Mum's rhubarb glut inspired me to cook some up with strawberries and then turn it into a purée. I love this as a cordial, topped with some sparkling water and ice – when you add the carbonated water to it, it creates an insane-looking foam. It's also good drizzled over vanilla ice cream.

Strawberry & rhubarb syrup

Makes 400ml (14fl oz)

100g (3½oz) granulated
  sugar
50ml (2fl oz) water
300g (10oz) rhubarb,
  chopped
300g (10oz) strawberries,
  hulled and halved
few drops of rosewater
  (optional)

1 Place the sugar and measurement water in a heavy-based saucepan and melt the sugar gently over a low heat, stirring often.

2 Add the rhubarb and strawberries and whack up the heat to medium-low. Cook the fruit for 20 minutes, then add the rosewater, if using, and cook for another 5 minutes.

3 Don't strain the syrup as it is the pulp that will make the drink foam up nicely. Pour it into a sterilized bottle or jar and seal until ready to use.

Buckthorn is becoming fashionable at places like Michelin-starred restaurant Noma in Copenhagen, where they serve it as a drink. We grew up with these berries, which you can find growing wild everywhere. The flavour is hard to describe – the berries are slightly bitter and sour, but they become refreshing when mixed with a little bit of orange rind and juice.

Обліпиха | *Oblipykha*
Buckthorn purée

**Makes a 350ml
(12fl oz) jar**

300g (10oz) buckthorn berries
300g (10oz) golden caster sugar
grated rind and juice of 1 orange

1 Blitz all the ingredients in a food processor and then pass the mixture through a sieve.

2 Transfer to a sterilized 350ml (12fl oz) jar, seal and keep in the refrigerator for up to 1 week. We use a spoonful of it in tea or added to a cold summer punch.

We make this when there is a glut of fruit. Whenever you have fruit or berries that are on the turn (anything except bananas), don't throw them away – slice them up and make this. Traditionally, we sweeten it with sugar, but I much prefer maple syrup or honey.

Компот | *Kompot*
Summer fruit punch

Makes 1.5 litres (2½ pints)

250g (8oz) strawberries, hulled
150g (5oz) buckthorn berries or
  gooseberries or chunks of rhubarb
175g (6oz) raspberries
100g (3½oz) blackberries
100g (3½oz) pears, pips and all, sliced
100g (3½oz) apples, pips and all, sliced
200g (7oz) white peaches, stoned
  and sliced
2 litres (3½ pints) cold water
75g (3oz) clear honey or maple syrup
ice and mint leaves, to serve

1 Place all the fruit in a large saucepan and cover with the water. Bring to the boil, then lower the heat and simmer for 30–45 minutes.

2 Stir in the honey or maple syrup, then strain and discard the fruit. Chill in the refrigerator, then serve in a jug with ice and mint.

Russians drink tea, while Ukrainians drink their fruit: *kompot* juices in the summer and *uzvars* in winter. This is my more decadent, spicy version of the traditional drink.

Uzvar | *Uzvar*
Winter punch

Makes 1.5 litres (2½ pints)

300g (10oz) dried apple slices
300g (10oz) dried apricots
300g (10oz) dried pitted prunes
200g (7oz) dried sour cherries
1 old, dried vanilla pod, without seeds
2 star anise
1 cinnamon stick
a few strips of lemon and orange rind
clear honey, to taste
3 litres (5¼ pints) cold water

1 Mix everything together in a large saucepan and cook over a low heat for 1 hour.

2 Strain the fruit and spices out (blitz the fruit without the spices in a food processor and serve with yogurt, porridge or rice pudding), cover and refrigerate until ready to drink. It will keep for up to 2 weeks and is amazing drunk warm with a shot of brandy.

This is a lot easier to do than fermenting your own fruit wine and a great way to use up a glut of fruit if you grow your own. The results are beautiful and it keeps for a long time. Again, your options are endless: you can use any flavoursome berry or apricots (halved and stoned), although I love fishing the blackcurrants out of my glass. My father distills his own vodka, but if you don't have enterprising parents, then any good-quality vodka will do.

Горілка | *Horilka*

Blackcurrant vodka

Makes 2 litres (3½ pints)

1kg (2lb) blackcurrants
250g (8oz) granulated
  sugar
500ml (17fl oz) good-
  quality vodka

1 Wash the blackcurrants and take them off their stalks, discarding any damaged currants.

2 Mix the currants with the sugar and vodka, then divide between a couple of sterilized 1 litre (1¾ pint) bottles or carafes.

3 Seal and leave to infuse for a month or so. It will keep for a year, if you don't drink it earlier.

A shot or two of this after a late lunch has always been excused by my Aunt Zhenia, who joked that this drink by nature contains a lot of micronutrients. It takes a month or so for the fruit to produce alcohol, when the fermentation will slow down. Berries with a lot of fibre (like blackcurrants) will take almost twice as long to ferment as berries with little fibre (raspberries), the latter will also produce more yield. You can make raspberry (*see* below), sour cherry, blackberry, blackcurrant or blueberry wine, too. Simply swap the berries in the recipe – the proportion of sugar stays roughly the same. Blackcurrant (*see* right) is my favourite though.

Смородинова мікро-елементи | *Smorodynovi mikro-elementy*
Blackcurrant micronutrients

Makes about 500ml (17fl oz)

1kg (2lb) fresh blackcurrants or raspberries
400g (13oz) granulated sugar

1 Make sure you discard any damaged blackcurrants or raspberries, and then crush the good ones with a potato masher or a fork.

2 Mix the crushed berries with the sugar in a container and leave in a warm place in the kitchen, covered by a muslin cloth until the fruit sinks to the bottom and you can see alcohol bubbles, stirring from time to time with a clean wooden spoon. This could take up to 2 weeks.

3 Place a fine sieve lined with a muslin cloth over a large container and strain the fruit out, pressing it with a wooden spoon or squeezing with clean hands.

4 Fill a sterilized glass jar with the strained liquid right to the top so that there is no air in the jar. Cover with a lid in which you have made a hole. Place some water in another smaller sterilized jar and connect it to the larger jar with a length of plastic tubing, fitting it through the hole in the lid. This is called a water stopper and is used to make sure the wine does not oxidize.

5 Leave the wine to ferment at 20–25°C (68–77°F) for 6 weeks (or 3 weeks if using raspberries), during which time the natural yeast will sink to the bottom. When you see this forming, pour off the liquid and discard the residue, then return the liquid to the jar. Repeat this process once or twice until the residue stops from forming and the liquid is no longer cloudy.

6 Decant the wine into a sterilized carafe or bottle, seal it and store in a cool, dark place – it should keep unopened for up to a year. Serve as a digestif in a shot glass after lunch or dinner.

Kvas is a non-alcoholic Russian fermented rye bread drink. When cold it can be as refreshing as cider or, indeed, blonde beer with a slice of lemon in it. It also has affinity with one of the most ancient drinks known to man – mead. The best *kvas* is made with natural yeast. The babushka I met at Kakhovka's market made it by mixing hop flowers with flour and hot water, which was then rolled into pellets and left to dry in the sun. Of course, you can use commercial, fresh yeast instead.

Хлібний квас | *Khlibnyy kvas*
Russian fermented rye drink

Makes 3 litres (5¼ pints)

200g (7oz) dried rye bread crusts (darker bread will produce a more complex flavour)
3 litres (5¼ pints) hot water
2 teaspoons caraway seeds, toasted and ground
1 teaspoon coriander seeds, toasted and ground
4 tablespoons raw honey or other good-quality honey
100g (3½oz) raisins
30g (1oz) natural yeast or 10g (⅓oz) fresh yeast or 5g (¼oz) dried active yeast
fresh mint or lemon verbena, to serve

1 Preheat the oven to 200°C/400°F/gas mark 6.

2 Place the rye bread crusts on a baking sheet and bake for about 30 minutes or until they turn dark and are completely dry.

3 Pop the baked crusts into a 3 litre (5¼ pint) sterilized jar and pour over the hot water. Add the ground caraway seeds and coriander seeds, cover with muslin and leave in a warm place for 2 days.

4 Strain the mixture through a clean muslin cloth, discard the bread and spices, then pour this bready water (called *suslo*) back into the jar. Add the honey, raisins and yeast, cover with clean muslin and leave to ferment for a day in a warm, dark place.

5 Pour the *kvas* into sterilized bottles, seal and leave to ferment for a further 6 hours in a warm, dark place. Place in the refrigerator to stop the fermentation. Serve cold with fresh mint leaves or lemon verbena.

6 If you enjoyed the drink, keep the sediment from the bottom of the bottles – you can add it to your next batch and the flavour will gradually become more and more complex.

Індекс | Index

A

apple
  in fruit punch 227
  sponge 196–7
apricots
  with Azerbaijani lamb 120
  baked cheese cake 194
  & gooseberry jam 171
  jam 172–3
  pyrizhky filling 56
  & sour cherry pie 214–15
  steamed dumplings 189
  Ukrainian biscotti 184–5
  winter punch 227
Armenian recipes
  beans with egg & herbs 89
  beans with tomato dressing 70–1
  cold yogurt & sorrel soup 36–7
  pickled vegetables 154–5
  pickled wet garlic 153
  roasted vegetables 74–5
  soup with lamb & prune
    meatballs 34–5
aubergine
  grilled rolls 72–3
  grilled vegetable 'caviar' 64–5
  sour 150–1
Azerbaijani recipes
  chicken with prunes & walnuts 124–5
  chickpea & mutton soup 32–3
  rice & fruity lamb 120–1
Azerbaydzhans'kyy plov 120

B

bacon, in cheese twist 52
banosh 117
barbecue
  catfish 140–1
  Causasian flatbreads 60
  kefir & herb chicken 132–3
barberries 84
beans, kidney, Georgian salad 68–9
beans, runner/French
  with egg & herbs 89
  Armenian beans with tomato
    dressing 70–1
  Armenian pickle 154

bear meat 135
beef
  spicy Georgian soup 28
  stock 12, 16, 23, 28
  stuffed cabbage leaves 84–5
beetroot
  Armenian pickle 154–5
  cold soup 18–19
  & gherkin salad 78–9
  leaves 15
  in pickled garlic 153
  & prune salad 66–7
  Ukrainian broth 12–13
Berlins'ke pechyvo 180
beshbarmak 114
birthday cake
  ice cream & strawberry 200–1
  Napoleon cake 187–8
biscotti, Ukrainian 184–5
biscuits, Berlin curd cheese 180–1
biskvit 197
blackberries
  sauce 176–7
  steamed dumplings 189
  summer fruit punch 227
blackcurrant
  leaves 8, 152, 154
  micronutrients 230–1
  vodka 228–9
borshch 12–13, 14–15, 159
bread
  fermented rye drink 233
  Ukrainian Easter 218–19
  Ukrainian garlic 42–3
  see also flatbread
brine 135, 148
broth
  campfire mutton 29
  chicken, with dumplings 24–5
  gherkin, beef & barley 16–17
  mushroom with buckwheat
    20–1
  piquant Russian 22–3
  sorrel 14–15
  Tsar's surf & turf 38–9
  Ukrainian beetroot 12–13
  see also soup

buckthorn
  purée 224
  summer fruit punch 227
buckwheat
  with chicken liver 126–7
  with mushroom broth 20–1
buns
  Ukrainian stuffed 54–7
  wasp nest 192–3
buzhenyna 135

C

cabbage
  Armenian pickle 154
  beetroot broth 12
  roasted 74
  slaw with toasted sunflower
    seeds 90–1
  sour 148–9
  stuffed leaves 84–5
  stuffed pasta 106
cakes
  apple sponge 196–7
  honey 198–9
  ice cream & strawberry 200–1
  Napoleon cake 187–8
  poppy seed roll 210–11
  Prague cake 206–8
  Ukrainian cheese cake 194–5
carrots
  Armenian roasted vegetables 74
  aromatic roast pork 135
  in broth 12, 15, 16, 23, 24, 28, 39
  in cabbage slaw 90–1
  Korean 88
  mutton in coriander 123
  in potato cakes 83
  with sour aubergine 151
  in sour cabbage 148
catfish, BBQ 140–1
Caucasian barbecue flatbreads
  60–1
cauliflower, Armenian roasted
  vegetables 74
Central Asian chicken & pasta
  114–15
chebureky 58

Індекс | Index

Індекс | Index

Подяки | Acknowledgements

Before I begin I would like to thank my dad Petro and my mum Olga for everything that they have done for me. As much as I love my little Kakhovka, Ukraine, I would have never been able to see the world and do the things that I have done and tell this story if it wasn't for their hard work and their love. You have given me such a strong core and such a huge appreciation of family. One of the hardest things I have to deal with every day is being so far away from you and the rest of our crazy *simiyka* Adamsiv aka the Adams family.

I would then like to thank my agent Ariella Feiner for noticing my work. I will never forget that very first email you've sent me. I immediately phoned my family and said I just knew that something miraculous was soon to happen.

Thank you also to Eve O'Sullivan, an amazing editor and writer at the *Guardian* for her enthusiasm for my mother's recipes which I first (gingerly) supplied and then got more and more encouraged to explore. Also a huge thank you must go to the brilliant Michail Tait, who spotted and loved my chicken tabaka video and raved to everyone about it. You have all in quick succession led me to the most incredible publishers in the industry.

Stephanie Jackson, our first meeting actually came at a painfully tough time for me. Your elative positivity and kindness have given me strength and self-belief that I thought I may have been losing. Thank you for digging my style and letting me write organically without trying to be anything that I wasn't.

Sybella Stephens, thank you for your input and constant support, you have been encouraging and insightful, someone a first-time writer could only dream to work with. Juliette Norsworthy, thank you for being so patient and for your insanely hard work, and for letting me inject even more of my vision into this project. Jo Richardson, Grace Helmer and the rest of the Octopus team, you have helped me create something so personal and so true, I never thought that was even possible. Thank you for going with the vibe and for producing something as incredible as this.

Kris Kirkham, you are not just a talented photographer. You are now one of my closest friends. You said you left a part of your heart in Ukraine and I think it was mutual. Thank you for seeing it through my eyes and thank you for loving it and for making my family feel so comfortable and happy especially when the situation in Ukraine was so devastatingly sad and uncomfortable.

Linda Berlin, thank you for helping me carry that buzz we started with Kris in Ukraine and transcending it into a studio in London.

Diana Henry, thank you for letting us use your beautiful house and for all of the energy and casual swearing. You know how much I love a spicy conversation.

Rosie Reynolds, thank you for your push with my styling career when I went solo. I will never forget your kind help when I needed it so badly. Thank you for keeping the photoshoots sane and for picking up things like the 2kg of crayfish by the London Zoo without blinking an eyelid. You are the coolest scouser and one of the best food stylists that I know.

A special thank you goes to my extended family in Ukraine. This book is yours. Aunt Lyuda, thank you for helping me bring Lusia and Zhenia's recipes back to life. Thank you for putting up with my annoying scales and my pathetic measuring spoons. Sorry we nearly made you faint in that heat, you are one of the best cooks that I know. Thank you Aunt Nina for all your Armenian and Azerbajani recipes and above all for your breath-taking stories, I can't stop thinking about your childhood in Karabakh, it is so mind-blowingly inspiring. Irochka, thank you for sending me Zhenia's recipes during the most devastating time of your life. Thank you to all of my family in Odessa, especially Lenochka.

Thank you to my beloved brother Sasha, his wife Alyona and the kids (especially Danila) for helping me test. Thank you to my beautiful babushka Vera and Aunt Valya for their Uzbeko-Russian feast. Poor gluten-free Kris said your *beshbarmak* was worth the pain. Babushka, you are one of the strongest women I know, you are simply my hero.

Thank you to all of the lovely people we encountered at the Kakhovka market and beyond. It just made me feel so proud to be part of such a friendly, beautiful, open people. I really hope I am doing you proud.

Thank you to all of my best friends in London and beyond. Caroline, Emma, Eve (again) thank you for your support with the testing. Emma the dough explosion in your fridge will forever make me chuckle. Eve, your mum devouring the whole of Napoleon made me the happiest woman alive.

Rachel thank you for giving me Sweetapple work when times were super tough. Eleanor, Jimmy, thank you for being there always.

Thank you to everyone who has helped me look after my son. Caroline, Colin, Reggie and Dotty, you are my family. I am so lucky I have you in my life.

Caroline, Terry, Ira and of course the Catley family – especially Julietta and Tim – thank you for holding my back when I had to carry on and work hard.

Finally, thank you Tom Catley, you have been an incredible inspiration for the past four years and you have given me my little Sasha aka Sashimi. Without you, Sashims, I do not think I would have pushed this hard to succeed. This is for you from your mama and three generations of mamushkas.

Olia Hercules was born in Ukraine and lived in Cyprus for 5 years before moving to London to study a BA in Italian, followed by an MA in Russian and English. A number of jobs followed before her interest in food as an amateur reached its apogee and she decided to retrain as a chef at Leith's School of Food and Wine. She kicked off her culinary career working at London's Union Market before landing her dream job as a chef-de-partie for Ottolenghi's. After having her son, and filming for The Food Network, Olia began writing for Sainsbury's, The Recipe Kit, and the *Guardian*. Find out more about Olia at oliahercules.com.